Electroni
Compu

New Directions in
Computers and Composition Studies

Gail H. Hawisher and Cynthia L. Selfe, Series Editors

Electronic Writing Centers:
Computing the Field of Composition

by

David Coogan
Illinois Institute of Technology

Ablex Publishing Corporation
Stamford, Connecticut

Printed in the United States of America

Library of Congress Cateloging-in-Publication Data

Coogan, David.
    Electronic writing centers : computing the field of composition
/ by David Coogan.
        p. cm.—(New directions in computers and composition studies)
    Includes bibliographical references and index.
    ISBN 1-56750-428-0 (cloth).—ISBN 1-56750-429-9 (pbk.)
    1. English language—Rhetoric—Study and teaching—Data
processing. 2. English language—Composition and exercises—Data
processing. 3. Report writing—Study and teaching—Data processing.
4. English language—Computer-assisted intruction. 5. Report
writing—Computer-assisted instruction. 6. Writing centers—
Automation. I. Title. II. Series: New directions in computers
and composition studies.
PE1404.C6347   1999
808'.042'0785—dc21   98-55723
                                                           CIP

Ablex Publishing Corporation
100 Prospect Street
P.O. Box 811
Stamford, Connecticut 06904-0811

Contents

Acknowledgments

This book began when I was a graduate student at the State University of New York at Albany. It emerged slowly, in the usual ways, first as course papers, then as conference presentations at CCCC, and then in journal articles (1994, 1995). But it emerged most intensely and most clearly to me not while I sat in front of my word processor, but during those earlier moments when I grew unusually attached to what was happening on my computer screen: those first moments of email "tutoring," working with students I couldn't see, sending messages back and forth for days, hoping, strategizing, to keep the conversation going. The excitement was not so much with email, I don't think, but with the ways in which email seemed to embody a particular vision of the future for writing centers, computers and composition, and their place in the larger discipline of Composition Studies; a future that I felt could be defined less by the containment of writing "problems" and more by the dialogic interplay between writers. It is that future, which is by no means a foregone conclusion, that I try to articulate in this book.

When I finished the first version of *Electronic Writing Centers*, as a dissertation, I did what I suspect is rather common. I graduated with little fanfare, packed up my belongings in a U-HAUL truck, and moved to another city to get ready for my first teaching job. Although the act of moving certainly gave me a sense of closure, the real closure came a year later in Logan, Utah, at the Computers and Writing Conference, where I was fortunate enough to receive The 1996 Hugh Burns Dissertation Award. Standing at the podium to receive the award not only gave me a sense of completion but a sense of achievement. But that closure, in fact, turned out to be another opening when, during that same weekend, Cynthia Selfe and Gail Hawisher asked me if I would be interested in publishing a revised version of the dissertation in their series, New Directions in Computers and Composition Studies. I was very interested.

To properly account for the origins of this work, then, I need to return to that first version of it and thank my dissertation committee—Steve North, Lil Brannon, and Ted Jennings. More than any others, they helped me shape these ideas at the point of utterance in their classes, in the hallways of the English department, on email, in their offices. I will always be grateful for their attention to my work. Next, I would like to thank Gail and Cindy for giving me just cause to revisit the dissertation. In that same vein, I would like to thank the anonymous reviewers at Ablex who helped me rethink the project as a book, with their perceptive and thorough comments. Thanks are also in order to the Department of Humanities, at Illinois Institute of Technology, for providing me with a summer-research fellowship.

But the greatest thanks must go to those who gave less directly but no less importantly: to the students whose writings appear in this book: without them there would be no book; to my wife, who gave me crucial feedback when I needed it most; to my mother, a kindergarten teacher, who shared with me her love of open-ended exploration in the classroom; to my grandmother, who coined the phrase "Just do it!" long before Nike and, more important, inspired me to do the same with these revisions; and to my father. Though he probably didn't realize it, I was watching him as he drafted his business reports and proposals at home, watching and learning from the extraordinary persistence, care, and focus that he brought to the act of writing. This book is dedicated to him.

Foreword

These days, it's hard not to be overwhelmed by the sheer number of articles in the popular and professional press that focus on technology in one of its many forms. Dozens of print magazines and hundreds of electronic publications explore the impact of personal computing technologies in our daily lives, and our water-cooler conversations are routinely filled with references to such things as the Y2K problem, the latest lawsuit against Microsoft, the newest microprocessor from Intel, the Communications Decency Act, and which website can give the most complete stats on Mark McGwire or Sammy Sosa. Whether canonized or demonized, blamed for its excesses or praised as a panacea to cure all social ills, the personal computer revolution is perceived with virtually no dissenting voices to be one of the most powerful social and cultural forces operant in our society, and nowhere is that power and force being felt more strongly at present than in the field of education.

With the recent formation of several virtual university consortiums such as Western Governors University, the Southern Regional Electronic Campus, and the Community College Distance Learning Network, it is increasingly evident that educational institutions are now beginning to see the Internet as an important resource for instructional delivery, a way to provide expanded learning opportunities and degree programs to many non-resident and/or non-traditional student populations. But the potential benefits of programs such as these, managed and coordinated through an environment that is almost entirely virtual and online, are not immediately apparent or sufficiently persuasive to all teachers, all students, or even all administrators. Many people are understandably wary of these environments and concerned about the quality of interactions which can take place between instructors and students, interactions that to many comprise the very essence of a quality education.

In this book, Dave Coogan uses his own experiences tutoring in one of these virtual educational environments, an online writing center, to argue that rich, high-quality interactions between instructors and students can indeed take place, despite the distance in space and time that separates them. Beginning his text with an argument that our thinking about both writing centers and instructional technologies has long been constrained by inappropriate metaphorical models (an argument supported by historical as well as theoretical evidence), Coogan makes a convincing case that we must apply an alternative, Bakhtinian framework to our understanding of these institutional and cultural artifacts in order to assess their interactions effectively. Using the e-mail tutoring sessions he had with his students at SUNY Albany about their drafts-in-progress as a series of miniature case studies, Coogan not only offers us a richly textured window into the problems and promise of this new medium, but he also illustrates how his proposed framework can structure our interpretations of the dialogically-based instructional moments that occur within it. Not content with making this point alone, Coogan extends it even further, going on to consider ways in which the critical literacy skills, fostered by this deeply interactive environment, can transform our views, and our students' views, of what education, teaching, and writing instruction are all about.

Though some people may not be convinced by Coogan's closing predictions about the effects of online tutoring on the overall educational mise-en-scène, everyone will be forced to reflect upon them seriously. I have had to, and I have gained a great deal from the experience. I'm certain that the rest of his readers will profit tremendously as well.

Michael A. Pemberton
University of Illinois, Urbana-Champaign

Introduction

Although peer tutoring programs and various configurations of networked writing classrooms have become ubiquitous in many college writing programs and English departments, the fields of writing centers and computers and composition have been largely unexplored in relation to the larger discipline of Composition Studies. In some cases, the absence is understandable, particularly in studies of our curricular and institutional history where the emphasis is upon an era that largely, but not completely, predates the mature development of these fields as fields with bodies of literature. In other cases, where the historical emphasis *is* upon the process era and its aftermath—the era that I, too, will also explore in this book—the absence is unexplainable.

When references to alternative scenes of teaching do appear, authors tend to discuss either tutoring or computing, but rarely both at the same time. For example, when Nancy Welch (1997) re-examined the concept of revision and took issue with the pedagogical drive toward closure and clarity, she discussed student writings in classrooms and in the writing center, but she did not discuss student writings online. Conversely, while Lester Faigley (1992) used postmodern theory to push Composition beyond the impasse between expressivism and constructivism, he identified the "achieved utopia" of networked writing only with classrooms, not with writing centers. Of course, there are exceptions. David Russell (1991) briefly mentioned both writing labs and computer labs in his massive curricular history of WAC, and several contributors to the anthology, *Writing Centers in Context,* edited by Joyce Kinkead and Jeanette Harris (1993), also explore the intersection between the two fields. But well-read anthologies such as Patricia Harkin and John Schilb's (1991) *Contending with Words,* or Richard Bullock, Charles Schuster, and John Trimbur's (1991) *The Politics of Writing Instruction: Postsecondary* contain no essays that devote more than a passing reference to computing or tutoring.

Admittedly, it is unfair to single out authors and editors for not addressing topics that they did not intend to address. Likewise, my brief survey of books and anthologies neglects those works devoted exclusively either to writing centers or computers and composition: for example, Christina Haas's (1996) *Writing Technology: Studies on The Materiality of Literacy;* Gail Hawisher and Cynthia Selfe's (1991) *Evolving Perspectives on Computers and Composition Studies: Questions For The 1990s,* Gary Olson's (1984) *Writing Centers: Theory and Administration*; and Muriel Harris' (1982) *Tutoring Writing: A Sourcebook for Writing Labs.* Nor has this growing body of scholarship been confined to books. Since the early 1980s, both fields have established their own journals—*Writing Center Journal, Writing Lab Newsletter, Computers and Composition, Kairos*—and their own professional societies, including the National Writing Centers Association and the Alliance for Computers and Writing. Yet despite this growth—or perhaps because of it—both fields have had little to say to each other and even less to say to the larger discipline of Composition Studies.

"Why," for example, asks Nancy Grimm (1996), "do we hear so little from writing centers in composition forums?" (p. 546). In part, she says, the silence has to do with the identification of writing centers and, I would add, computers and composition, with strictly practical or non-scholarly matters; as support services or, in the case of computer labs, mere utilities that are only worth discussing when service is interrupted. As a result, when scholars present histories of the discipline, and researchers present studies of writers writing, or teachers present new pedagogies, they consistently foreground what Charlie Moran (1992) calls "the brick and mortar classroom." Through sheer repetition, this space becomes a natural space—really, the only space—where instruction officially takes place. When chairpersons, deans, and tenure review committees examine the work of teachers outside these spaces, they inevitably have the brick-and-mortar classroom in mind as a point of comparison: How many tutoring hours make up a three credit class? At what point in a computer classroom does the teacher lecture (that is, *really* teach?). The waters become even muddier when areas of teaching, service, and research begin to blur, as is often the case in writing centers and computers and composition. For example, when someone establishes a peer-tutor training course, should this be considered under service or teaching? When a technorhetorician teaches her colleagues how to use computers in a writing class, and subsequently does a study on computer-mediated teaching, should this be considered under service or research?

These scenarios only become serious problems, I might add, when writing centers and computers and composition are rendered invisible or inconsequential by their service—when they are construed narrowly as adjuncts to the real classroom, as if these fields had nothing else to offer but service. While it may be true, of course, that many practitioners in these areas are content to serve in a supportive capacity, Grimm (1996), at least, makes clear that writing centers do not always hail themselves this way. Even as they attempt to situate their work in broader, theoretical contexts, writing centers are expected to *deal* with "students who speak English as a second language, students who use a nondominant dialect, students who have learning disabilities, students who don't follow assignment guidelines" (p. 524), and so on. In what amounts to a double standard, she says, writing centers are expected "to master and control this heterogeneity rather than interpret it" (p. 524) for the discipline. They are expected to play the part that has been constructed for them, but they are not expected to do much more, for example, to tell their own story about their work in the discipline.

Take, for example, the way writing centers and computers and composition fit into the now-familiar story of the process revolution, as told by Maxine Hairston (1982). In her much-discussed essay, "The Winds of Change: Thomas Kuhn and the Revolution in the Teaching of Writing" Hairston announced to readers of *College English* that the current–traditional paradigm, with its perennial focus on usage, style, and the composed product had finally collapsed. Many forces, she said, had exhausted the old paradigm, including "open admissions policies, the return to school of veterans and other groups of older students who are less docile and rule-bound than traditional freshman, the national decline in conventional verbal skills, and the ever larger number of high school graduates going on to college" (p. 82). What really failed, however, in Hairston's view, was not so much current–traditional rhetoric but practitioners of current–traditional rhetoric: "untrained teachers" in English departments with "little scholarly interest" (p. 82) in the teaching of writing. According to Hairston, these teachers were simply ill-equipped to handle new challenges in the teaching of writing—ill-equipped and, perhaps, indifferent.

A curious feature of the argument, then, is this ambivalence toward practitioners. Though she doesn't exactly blame them for promoting "a static and unexamined approach to teaching writing," (p. 79) she clearly does not exonerate them: "the majority of college writing teachers in the United States are not professional writing teachers. They do not do research or publish on rhetoric or composition, and they do not know the scholarship in the field" (p. 79). Though she assures us that a process revolution *is* at hand—that winds of change *are* sweeping the nation—it is clearly not a revolution in practice but a revolution in theory, as Hairston makes clear through her review of research by Lester Faigley, Stephen Witte, Linda Flower, John Hayes, Sondra Perl, Sharon Pianko, Nancy Sommers, and others. Practitioners in writing centers and computers and composition, not surprisingly, got the short end of the stick in this formulation of revolution. To Hairston, they were merely part of "the transition period" between the old product paradigm and the new process paradigm:

> Following the pattern that Kuhn describes in his book, our first response to crisis has been to improvise *ad-hoc* measures to try to patch the creaks and keep the system running. Among the first responses were the writing labs that sprang up about ten years ago to give first aid to students who seemed unable to function within the traditional paradigm. Those labs are still with us, but they're still giving only first aid and treating symptoms. They have not solved the problem. Another *ad hoc* remedy took the form of individualized instruction, but it has faded from the scene along with computer-assisted instruction. The first was too costly and too isolated, the second proved too limited and impersonal. (p. 82)

This characterization of writing center work drew immediate criticism from Stephen North (1984), who noted in his landmark essay "The Idea of the Writing Center" that Hairston, unfairly, had engaged a rhetoric of blaming the victim: "The implication is that 'they' done it—'they' being, apparently, the places themselves" (p. 437). North's point was that the current–traditional mandate to straighten out snarled syntax did not stem from the writing center community but "clearly from the sponsoring body, usually an English department" (p. 437).

Although this may appear to be a trivial point—and an old one, at that—I believe it is worth unpacking at some length. At stake, it would seem, is a politics of remediation *within* Composition Studies, formulated at a time when leading practitioners in the field, such as Donald Murray (1976), publicly vowed to "teach process not product" and leading theorists established competing methodological camps to study the composing process. In his book-length study of those competing methodologies, North (1987) argued that the integrity of the discipline, as a knowledge-making enterprise, is premised upon the "concerted divestiture of the Practitioners" (p. 337). In order to credit themselves with the making of knowledge in composition, scholars and researchers had to discredit practitioners, in the classroom and in the writing center. To say, then, that practitioners in writing centers or computers and composition kept the current–traditional paradigm standing, at a time when others had determined that the foundation had cracked, wrongly absolves not just English departments but a whole host of stakeholders that were instrumentally involved in sustaining what I will call an Ideological State Apparatus (ISA) of functional literacy.

The premise that I take up in Chapter One, then, is that revolution in the new *discipline* was soiled by a far less revolutionary urge to contain—not current-traditional rhetoric—but functional literacy in the *field*. If the effort to contain writing problems then became an embarrassment to Composition—anathema to its disciplinary ambitions—it also became a well-concealed embarrassment. The tactic, then and now, has been to cloak the ISA of literacy as current–traditional rhetoric, often by invoking Thomas Kuhn's (1962) idea of the paradigm shift. Although critiques of the paradigm argument have been made already (e.g., Knoblauch, 1984; North, 1987), the idea of an old, current–traditional, period remains, in many ways, an irresistible other—an uncontainable, unthinking force that, like nuclear waste, could, at any moment, contaminate the purity of the modern discipline. The implied hostility toward practitioners—part-timers, adjuncts, tutors, and technorhetoricians—is barely contained in this formulation. The term "traditional" allows us locate the problem in the past—with school marms or the inflexible handbooks that they used—all the while warning us that, perhaps, things haven't really changed. Somewhere, some teacher, tutor, or computer program is marking up essays in dehumanizing, ineffective ways; somewhere, some chairperson, dean, or administrator is getting ready to hire practitioners or buy remedial grammar programs to get the job done.

Misconceptions of current–traditional rhetoric would not be so important if the term was not used, in a pivotal sense, to absolve the discipline from any further consideration of functional literacy in our present relations. In the first chapter, I re-tell the story of Composition in the 1960s, '70s, and '80s, paying special attention to those often inconspicuous relations between program administrators, corporations, government agencies, researchers, and faculty—relations that created the isolated, remedial lab and the cure-all teaching machine. Changing those relations and thus the direction of the discipline does not seem possible, however, unless we are able to identify the apparatus with certain administrative, technological, and pedagogical formations, that is, until we can identify functional literacy with something else besides textbook publishing trends and the legacy of a fallen Rhetoric. "Indeed," as Louis Althusser points out in his discussion of ideological state apparatuses (1971), "the reality in question is the mechanism" itself—"the very forms of recognition" (p. 182) that interpellate the subject of composition.

In this mechanism, literacy becomes that illusory social glue that holds the idea of the university "community" together: It is the one experience that everyone is compelled to share, no matter what their interests in university education. Once students have passed this "basic" literacy test or taken the proper course, they are allowed to move through a general education program and then through a specialized degree program. Literacy becomes, in this sense, a pre-college skill or a rite of passage into higher education, but not a serious, or integral part of that education. The Strategy of Containment, likewise, assures Composition, the academic community, and other stakeholders such as English departments, that any writing problems that crop up after this progression has been set in motion will be contained, quietly and discreetly, in the writing center. Of course, tutorial conversations often stray considerably from the mediating function they purportedly serve, engaging instead a heteroglossia of competing intentions, accents, and meanings. Nevertheless, these conversations are often construed by others as remedial sessions on grammar or editing—conversations that have no real relationship to academic work.

Naturally, these assumptions continue to put many practitioners on the defensive. "What exactly is it writing centers do?," asks Muriel Harris (1990), in her best imitation of the academic community:

> Are we running only remedial centers, places to salvage some of the "boneheads" that have been permitted to enroll (for however brief a tenure) in our institutions? Are we band-aid clinics offering clean-up service for papers about to be handed in? Such questions persist with the tenacity of barnacles. We seem forever to be countering these and other equally limited notions. But why do we perennially have to keep explaining ourselves? And why do we keep doing it from a somewhat defensive posture? (p. 17)

These questions sting anyone who has ever worked in or supported a writing center not just because they can be insulting but because they seem perennial. Framed the way they usually are, as a problem of communication, it would seem that either the writing center has done a poor job with public relations, or the academic community has done a poor job of listening. Harris contends that part of the problem is with public relations, a case where writing center insiders have failed to relate their confidence in individualized instruction to larger communities. Among the many traditions that she identifies in this ten year retrospective on writing centers, the most alarming tradition is the one of mystifying our colleagues:

> This tradition of misunderstanding is so persistent that it isn't likely to disappear unless we address the composition community in ways we haven't yet done, for writing centers also have a tradition of not speaking up effectively. There have been endless calls for research in the writing center, to validate and elucidate what we do, and it is a tradition that we keep on making those calls—and not answering them. Far too little research, especially research that will wake up and inform our colleagues, has been conducted in our writing centers. And there have been far too few articles presenting general theories of individualized instruction. We have, in fact, talked too much to ourselves in our journals and at our conferences (and in those phone calls and visits) and not enough to the world of composition outside. (p. 18–20)

The solution to this dilemma, she argues, will not be found in more journal articles aimed at the writing center community. What's needed instead is a "more effective approach, stance, action, or method of explanation" (p. 20) aimed directly at the larger composition community. Harris's (1995) own attempt at such an explanation appeared several years later in *College English*.

Of course, in the isolationist mode—writing center vs. the composition community—the problem of communication appears insurmountable: What more could be said that hasn't already been said? The problem also seems oddly familiar. One hears in Harris's formulation an uncanny resemblance to the problems facing students, which writing centers know intimately well. The writing center (or student) feels unable to communicate effectively to Composition (her teacher) because they each have different perspectives, different needs, and apparently no common ground to resolve their problems. One of the reasons I've chosen to reject this formulation of the problem is that I want to relieve the writing center profession of the full burden of bridge work, much like I would relieve the student of the full burden of bridge work. In fact, I'm not sure the metaphor of building a bridge is even appropriate in the dialogic setting I am imagining for the electronic writing center.

This book, then, is not a call for writing centers to take on extra public relations work. Nor is it a call for more research to explain better what writing centers already do. It is a call for the entire composition community to coordinate a new mandate for the electronic writing center; to imagine an alternate future for peer tutors and the students that they serve, not by abandoning traditional writing centers but by enhancing them with electronic counterparts. Creating these counterparts means rethinking what Composition generally expects of writing centers and what writing centers generally expect of themselves. It also means rethinking the history of the process movement.

As Lester Faigley (1992) reminds us, the construction of individuality in higher education, so important in process pedagogies and student-centered conferencing, did not emerge in composition research alone, but in a larger context of 1960s campus radicalism, alongside the Students for a Democratic Society (SDS), the feminist movement, and civil rights activism. "What students cried out for" in the 1960s and 1970s was "autonomy, anti-authoritarianism, and personal voice" (p. 57). Early proponents of expressivism, for example, shared with SDS a "disdain for political quietism on college campuses" (p. 57); with feminists, they committed to consciousness raising, the sharing of personal narratives, and a critique of competitive, patriarchal discourse; and with civil rights activists, they politicized standard (white) English, defended the link between dialect and cultural heritage, and publicly resolved in a CCCC executive committee statement, "to respect diversity and uphold the right of students to their own language" (p. 60). These movements critiqued the normalizing function of the university and denied that students were merely passive recipients of education. In *The University in Ruins,* Bill Readings (1996), links these politics of individualism to a historical project of the modern university; a project that he feels has outlived its usefulness as the "grand narrative" of "self-finding," where the "subject of human history strives for autonomy, for the self-knowledge that will free it from the chains of the past" (p. 52). According to Faigley (1992), however, Composition sustains this narrative when it construes "the writer as an autonomous self" (p. 15) fully in control of his or her meaning, peddling into the wind, as it were, with nothing but "hard work aimed at producing an enduring object" (p. 191). This is not to say that enduring objects made of words have no value. Rather, the point is to question the relationship between essayist literacy and the status of a discipline charged with initiating newcomers to the ways and means of university life.

Knoblauch and Brannon (1993), for example, have argued that reform movements such as expressivism that emphasized the primacy of consciousness, were often incapable of studying or even acknowledging the larger "dynamics of institutional power" (p. 127). Classroom pedagogies such as freewriting, curricular initiatives such as whole language, and theoretical concepts such as voice, became possible "because they could be envisioned without serious challenge to the underlying political conditions" (p. 128) in the university. "Such programs," they suggest, "have become, in effect, the coffee breaks of the educational workforce" (p. 28). What this suggests is that if literacy instruction has not been radically changed by expressivism, it seems that the oppositional politics of individualism are in need of revision, not necessarily the spirit of reform that gave rise to those tactics.

For writing centers, part of this opposition has to do with the tenuous identity of peer tutors, who are often portrayed both as insiders *and* outsiders of the academic community; as liminal people with conditional status in the worlds of teachers and of students; as model "writers," on the one hand, and model students on the other hand. As insiders/students, peer tutors can "demystify the system," as Hawkins (1980) has argued, by representing a kinder, gentler version of the academic community. Yet as outsiders/writers, these same peer tutors can be comrades in struggle who share the same challenge of writing for teachers in a confusing, sometimes alienating, discourse. Others, of course, have taken a less conciliatory—but no more oppositional—stance to the status of peer tutors in the writing center. "In short," wrote North (1984) "we are not here to serve, supplement, back up, complement, reinforce, or otherwise be defined by any external curriculum. We are here to talk to writers" (p. 440). Anyone who has ever worked in a writing center knows why these positions are appealing. But, as Harris pointed out earlier, this rhetoric of autonomy can force others into ill-informed speculation about the writing center. The outsider image that is implied, ultimately, opposes the writing center to the university it serves, or worse, nurtures indifference amongst the staff and the faculty about the ways in which its "service" can be abused, symbolically and practically, by administrators, students, and faculty.

Some of this resistance, of course, continues to be well-placed. But so far as I can tell, what's needed now is not more generalizations of "the system" but a reshaping of ourselves in relation to the curricular systems that we inhabit: first year writing programs, WAC programs, undergraduate, and graduate degrees. What we need, in other words, are new forums for writing and reading that cut against the construction of heroic individualism and the equally restrictive construction of "community." We need to create electronic spaces that emphasize the individual's changing obligations to other writers—forums that enact dialogic literacy.

In Chapter Two, I identify email tutoring with this project, using Mikhail Bakhtin's work to define a new mandate for dialogic literacy in the center. What I admire most in Bakhtin's thinking, is his celebration of the self-in-relation to the other. For example, where many saw the other negatively in terms of alienation or miscommunication, Bakhtin (1990) saw it as a creative opportunity: "Only the other is capable of being formed and consummated *essentially*" (p. 188). If we take Bakhtin seriously in this passage, then we take seriously the responsibility to be open to the other or to risk a social death. What this amounts to, according to Bakhtin theorists and biographers, Katerina Clark and Michael Holquist (1984), is a "kind of epistemological mandate: 'To be means to communicate dialogically. When the dialogue ends, everything ends'" (p. 86).

In my discussion of email "tutoring," therefore, I celebrate the opportunity to pursue written dialogue, itself, as a form of literacy: to cultivate a respect for the incommensurable and tolerance of dissensus through extended online conferencing. I believe this form of interaction can help us rearticulate the subject in the writing center, by affording us the opportunity to value those off-stage voices and contradictory impulses that make up the undergraduate writer's (and tutor's) world. Where the traditional center uses speech to straighten-out writing, or clarify the writer's intentions in the context of the writer's own thought process and disciplinary expectations, the electronic center would use email and other forms of computer-mediated communication to complicate writing or sort through contradictory intentions. Where the traditional center construes peer tutors as coaches or mentors in the writing process, the electronic center would construe tutors as collaborators, co-writers, interpreters, and publishers of student writing. Where the traditional center defines itself in a supportive capacity, serving freshman writing programs, WAC programs, or the entire university community, the electronic writing center would serve groups of students, in synchronous or asynchronous time, by encouraging the creative juxtaposition or transformation of ideas. The central concept would not be the individual writer but the negotiating group; the pedagogical goal would not be fluency but answerability; the larger objective would not be autonomy but inter-dependence.

The mission of the electronic writing center (EWC), in other words, would not be to support the university curriculum or even to subvert it but to complicate its designs by critiquing the assumption that replication, imitation, and knowledge-telling (Flower, 1994) are sufficient rhetorical platforms for undergraduates; conversely, to critique the assumption that personal, non-academic writing is a sufficient form of resistance. The strategy would be to expand the audiences for student writing and, in this way, expand the possibilities of what might be said in a university community. In this way, perhaps, an EWC could also expand the very meaning of community, so that is not defined so narrowly by expertise, on the one hand, and general education, on the other hand; specialized ways of reading and writing, on the one hand, and generalizations of "basic" literacy or "personal" literacy on the other hand.

Clearly, this project calls into question the limits of our current debates over the subject. It also challenges what we mean by student-centered teaching in the writing center. Grimm (1996) identifies what appears to be at stake in any rearticulation of writing center work.

> If writing centers and composition studies want to make movement among communities more likely, they will need more complicated notions of subjectivity that allow for a self as always conflicted and under construction, yet at the same time a self capable of negotiating with subject positions offered by assignments and coerced by grading practices. If writing centers differentiate themselves and move out of the awkward triangulation between student and teacher, where they are expected not to change what students learn but to get students to conform to institutional expectations and values, they can become genuine spaces where students negotiate conflicts and where knowledge about the conflict among literacies can be generated and shared. (p. 530)

There are significant barriers, however, to the type of space Grimm imagines: an overcommitment to flexibility and service, resistance to theorizing, and lack of focus on developing a mission. Because this project involves technology, there is an additional concern. In order to avoid what I call a Rhetoric of Technocentrism,[1] or an unqualified faith in technological progress, we need to be careful not to link dialogic literacy absolutely with computing. As a corrective, then, or a sobering reminder of what is at stake, I discuss in Chapter Three two more email sessions that, in my view, re-assert old relations in the apparatus of functional literacy: sessions where tutors and students play more familiar roles fixing problems, intervening in the composing process, and trying to demystify academic discourse. The medium, I conclude, may not contain a message. But if we want students to engage the dialogic with email—to break the binary between "my own opinions" and "what the teacher wants," or the choice between writing close-to-the-self and writing in a disciplinary community—than I believe we will need a critical theory of technology that links the burden for change with people, not computers.

What else, then, can writing centers do to establish a critically reflexive presence online? In what ways can we confront the privacy of the one-to-one writing conference, the autonomy of the writer, and the legacies of containment and technocentrism? What is the idea of the electronic writing center? In order to answer this question, I have, in Chapter Four, taken a somewhat unusual approach. There, I revisit the sessions discussed in Chapters Two and Three and re-read them alongside and against other students' essays on similar topics—essays that I searched for and then downloaded from the Internet. I then go on to theorize the electronic writing center as a place on a wide-area network where it becomes possible and even natural for students to begin quoting other students, in and out of the tutorial, across course sections, disciplines, and semesters; a place where student writing can be read instead of graded; transformed instead of processed. If such work leads students to question the borders of knowledge in the university, to become "answerable," as Bill Readings (1996) puts it, "to the question of justice, rather than the criteria of truth," (p. 154), then the electronic writing center might go on to embody what writing centers have long promised to embody: a center for consciousness about writing in higher education, a (virtual) place where writers compose, collaborate, and find others who at different times, perhaps under different constraints, also engaged a similar activity.

Obviously, or so it seems to me, the projects that I am discussing represent opportunities for all stakeholders to resist the ISA of literacy. Though I cannot predict the outcomes or even the ultimate value of such resistance, my more limited point is that the relations that sustain functional literacy in higher education are not beyond our discernment and, hence, not beyond our control. They exist, among other places, in the ways we construct tutoring and computing in the discipline. By studying the history of writing centers and computers and composition, then, I believe one studies much more than the past but also those present relations that limit our progress toward dialogic literacy today. A critical review of our relations in the ISA of literacy becomes useful, then, insofar as it helps us to refigure an apparatus of dialogic literacy for Composition and for the academic communities it serves.

We know from scholars such as Henry Giroux that every curriculum has a hidden curriculum. Social relations may not be the subject of schooling but they are the ultimate product of what takes place there. In this book, I make explicit those relations that originally framed writing centers and computers and composition in order to reshape them along more generative lines. If I am right in assuming that literacy is not about timeless, arhetorical, skills but about intricate, dialogic connections with each other, then our challenge, as teachers, as scholars, and as administrators, is to match our understanding of dialogic literacy with reality, to find alternative ways of teaching writing in the university. That is, after all, what folks in writing centers and computers and composition tend to do best.

1

Tutors and Computers in Composition Studies

These are political choices: the question is, what indeed should students become and who should have the power to say so? What indeed should the nation aspire to, and who should compose the stories about that aspiration?
— (Knoblauch & Brannon, 1993, p. 6)

In the introduction, I suggested that what we usually describe as the old current–traditional paradigm is, in fact, best described as an ideological state apparatus of functional literacy. The shift in terminology from *paradigm* to *apparatus* is not merely semantic but strategic. It allows me to emphasize a social network of people and programs instead of a rhetorical tradition or a series of rhetoricians. It allows me to foreground those alliances between faculty, students, administrators, corporations, governments, and the general public that sustain the idea of literacy—alliances that are sometimes implicit and, as I will show in this chapter, sometimes explicit.

The notion that rhetoric and composition is enmeshed in such relations should not be surprising. Others have already invoked a larger politics of literacy operating in English Studies (Berlin, 1996; Miller, 1991; Ohmann, 1976), in the history of rhetoric (Kitzhaber, 1953; Knoblauch & Brannon, 1984; Miller, 1989), in the college curriculum (Geisler, 1994; Herzberg, 1991; Russell, 1991), and in American

1

culture (Knoblauch & Brannon, 1993; Stuckey, 1991; Trimbur, 1991). These works suggest that literacy has always been a contested space where Americans have attempted to regulate a national identity, as evidenced, for example, in the battery of composition courses and placement exams for "regular" students, "remedial" students, "honors" students, and "international" students—distinctions that still dominate many writing programs today.

Often missing or faintly drawn in these studies, however, are writing centers and computers and composition, two fields that I believe were instrumental in the disciplinary formation of Composition Studies. These fields were important not because they led the charge to "Teach Process!," but because they sustained the idea that functional literacy mattered, even to a profession that had, theoretically, washed its hands of it. The legacy of these disciplinary politics lives on, as I will suggest later, in a Strategy of Containment and a Rhetoric of Technocentrism, both of which locate writing problems in the non-disciplinary, or merely practical learning spaces of the writing lab and the computer lab.

Although the fields of writing centers and computers and composition, in some ways, have shaken loose these shackles of containment, they have not—and Composition has not—broken the locks. We are, in my opinion, still contained by these quick-fix assumptions because we have not radically reframed our relations of production in the apparatus of functional literacy: We have not changed the ways we construe tutoring and computing in Composition Studies. "We," as I have already suggested, does not refer to an anonymous group of power-brokers determined to keep these fields in their places. Nor does it refer to those who imagine themselves outside of this debate, who would deny their own complicity in these relations, locally or nationally. "We" refers to any teacher, administrator, professional, or researcher who made early teaching machines and writing labs a reality, directly or indirectly; who imagined, or continues to imagine, these spaces as solutions to "the literacy problem" in higher education.

In arguing for the durability and continuity of this apparatus, I don't mean to imply that there have been no substantial changes in writing centers and computers and composition over the last 30 years. I do, however, want to draw attention to the limitations of those changes, or what appears to be a default logic in Composition proper, that these fields could never be organizing principles for the discipline. In order to clearly imagine such a principle, I suggest first we need to acknowledge and then change the ways that we interpellate tutors and computers at the margin of the discipline. To begin, we might construe the history of both fields as something more than separate, unrelated histories; to re-situate the lore of tutoring and computing within the disciplinary ambition of Composition Studies. If I am right in assuming that these fields emerged in the shadow of process research, in its cognitivist and expressivist forms; that they sustained the idea that functional literacy mattered even to a discipline that was prepared to move on, then I will need to define the apparatus of functional literacy in more detail.

FUNCTIONAL LITERACY AS AN IDEOLOGICAL STATE APPARATUS

According to Cy Knoblauch and Lil Brannon (1993), "the most familiar, and probably the most popular 'representation' of literacy" in America (p. 17) is functional literacy. In this model, language is a "'code' that enables the 'processing' of 'information'; speakers and writers are 'encoders' and 'senders' of information-bearing 'messages,' while hearers and readers are 'receivers' and 'decoders'" (p. 17). The "ultimate value of language," they say "lies in its utilitarian capacity to pass information back and forth for economic or other material gain" (p. 18). Breakdowns, which inevitably occur, have little to do with language itself or the context of transmission; everything to do with the processing behavior of senders and receivers. (Pronoun disagreement between the singular and the plural <A person should do what they want> allegedly tells us more about the student's processing behavior than the student's ambivalence toward gender inclusive language.)

This focus on "processing behavior" is especially noteworthy in the context of American higher education, and not only in relation to gender issues. Perhaps the greatest appeal of functionalism is that it simultaneously locates communication problems "in" an individual, while assuming that all individuals are essentially the same—equipped, as it were, with the same language tools. If language is nothing but a tool, the authors say, then the purpose of language instruction is to learn how "to control the world of information for personal and social advantage" (p. 86). The image they use to describe this perspective is pure Americana: "The literate person is like Paul Bunyon, heroically self-reliant, an ax-wielder, a clearer of forests who creates the nation's material prosperity through technical know-how, determination, and hard work" (p. 86). In this context, functionalism becomes not just an approach to language, but an approach to the American melting pot, where all peoples are compelled to rise by the bootstraps of their "successful communication" in English.

Though there may be something curiously American about the concept of functional literacy, there is nothing mysterious about its origins in higher education. According to David Russell (1991) the idea of transportable writing skills—learned once and then applied to any situation—was inconceivable in the old liberal arts college of the 19th century. Before the 1870s, he says, when "writing was ancillary to speaking" colleges paid little attention to composition skills, because they knew that their graduates would be required to speak not write, "in the pulpit, the senate, and the bar" (p. 4). The purpose of college, however, was not to train students to enter these professions. Rather, colleges emphasized the "mental disciplines" of classical languages and philosophy, which were practiced through the rhetorical arts of recitation, oral examination, and debate. This type of education was designed for gentlemen who, by most accounts, expected to begin their careers after college with apprenticeships that were arranged through family connections. College and public schooling were not universal, nor were they egalitarian.

After 1870, however, when America had established "a host of new professions whose members communicated primarily through texts" (p. 4), the relationship between college, composition, and career would change. Writing, in the newly expanded university system, was no longer a preparation for public speaking but was instead "embedded in a whole array of complex and highly differentiated social practices carried on without face-to-face communication" (Russell, p. 4), practices that were, in fact, highly dependent upon new print technologies: "the modern pen, Linnotype, vastly improved presses, typewriter, duplicating machines, vertical files, etc." (p. 4). The emerging consensus that writing was merely transcribed speech, then, harkened back to the pre-disciplinary, liberal arts college that was actually much more dependent on speech.

Significantly, the association between writing and transcribed speech also harkened back, nostalgically, to a more homogenous, student body defined primarily by Anglo-Protestant men in the upper economic sphere. As Russell makes clear, the new universities of the modern era were not bound by pastoral, Christian sensibility, but by a respect for new knowledge and a utilitarian drive for upward mobility, as evidenced in the increasing number of graduate degree programs, accredited universities, and new students seeking higher education. If the old liberal arts college could accurately be described as a speech community, the new university could hardly be considered, in the same breath, as a writing community. As Russell points out, even professors found it increasingly difficult to understand each others' writings: "Faculty [in the new university] thought of their writing not as persuasive discourse, subject to the same rhetorical and stylistic analysis as a sermon or a campaign speech, but rather as an unproblematic rendering of the fruits of research" (p. 10).

What interests me about this history of higher education is the way professional, middle-class culture created the need for writing and reading instruction. I am especially interested in the way literacy became associated with upward mobility. As Russell pointed out, the struggle between the soul of the old liberal arts college and the prospects of the new research university was played out, and continues to be played out, in the general education curriculum, located almost exclusively in the first two years of college. To proponents of gen-ed, the point of these two years is to give the university experience some form of coherence. To proponents of specialization, the point is to inculcate in new students a respect for expert knowledge. As Cheryl Geisler (1994) notes in her book *Academic Literacy and the Idea of Expertise,* during this time, "professionals not only had to arrange the conditions for their own market advantage through a credential system, they also had to create the market for their professional services" (p. 80). In newly formed English departments devoted to Literature, the gen-ed movement materialized in introductory literature courses and lower-division writing courses. As Susan Miller (1991) points out in *Textual Carnivals: The Politics of Composition,* generalized writing instruction performed important ideological work in the discipline of English Studies: "the two pursuits of literature and composition were joined immediately as 'high' and 'low,' advanced and elementary. Equally to the point, they were one bourgeois effort at delight and instruction, leisure and work" (p. 53).

By banishing writing to the gen-ed curriculum, where it has floundered ever since, English departments, according to Miller, were then able to hail the new student as "a presexual, preeconomic, prepolitical person" (p. 87) incapable of serious, literary discourse—a person with only a functional need to control information; to "work" in other Philistine professions. By locating literacy in the gen-ed curriculum, English also affirmed what others had, perhaps, already assumed; that proper writing, like proper speaking, was a transportable "skill" learned once and easily applied to any situation. In more symbolic ways than actual ways, writing became the social glue that held together the idea of a university community, the one course that everyone, in the new elective system, shared—or was made to share.

Although this history has been well documented by Miller (1991), Connors (1983), Russell (1991), and others, I believe it is a history worth reflecting upon, if only to note the disbursement of responsibility and the creation of "need" in the student body. John Trimbur (1991) has suggested that the "rhetorical power of the phrase 'literacy crisis'", which is almost always invoked implicitly or explicitly in this context, "resides in its ability to condense a broad range of cultural, social, political, and economic tensions into one central image" (p. 277). It is an image, or a "discourse of crisis," that repeatedly links "middle class anxieties to nativist sentiments" (p. 293) about who "we" Americans really are and who "we" are not; a discourse that throughout history has revealed a "fear of the alien and the other—whether Irish Catholics in the 1840s, southern and Eastern Europeans in the 1890s, or Hispanics and Asians in the 1980s" (p. 293). This fear, which can be as subtle as it can be blunt, suggests that functional literacy "functions" as a cultural battleground not just in English departments but in America; that writing "skills" are not so easily abstracted from the writers who exercise those skills. The tendency, however, is toward abstraction, to promise undergraduates what we cannot, truthfully, ever deliver: the acquisition of communication skills that cut across differentials in race, gender, age, sexual orientation, power, and class; skills that grant the new student a place in "our" community.

The terms *infrastructure* and *superstructure*, as formulated by Louis Althusser (1971), become useful here insofar as they allow us to see functional literacy as something more than a personal preference in teaching or an abstract idea but as an ideological state apparatus (ISA)—an edifice constructed in word and action. The infrastructure, or the base of this edifice, includes the relations of production—conference hours, curricular structures, technologies, salaries, space allocations, and so on; while the superstructure includes those alliances that control the means of production. Such control is not purchased through violence or top-down expressions of power, but through ideological interpellation. As Althusser explains,

I shall then suggest that ideology 'acts' or 'functions' in such a way that it 'recruits' subjects among the individuals (it recruits them all), or 'transforms' the individuals into subjects (it transforms them all) by that very precise operation which I have called interpellation or hailing, and which can be imagined along the lines of the most commonplace everyday police (or other) hailing: 'Hey, you there!' (p. 174)

In colleges and universities, the student is hailed through placement tests, required freshmen writing courses, exit exams, referrals to the writing lab, and so on; hailed, that is, as a writer existing outside of history in a context-free environment. Even when writing programs attempt to circumvent this hail, by responding differently, say, with cultural studies anthologies in the first year writing course, or narrative-based portfolio exams, the siren continues to wail, and it is often answered by others. That is what I believe occurred in Composition Studies during the so-called disciplinary phase of growth and expansion during the 1960s and 1970s. Functional literacy was re-directed or pushed across *the field*, where it was picked up by writing labs and automated teaching machines. As I will suggest later, these relations were entrenched through a Strategy of Containment and a Rhetoric of Technocentrism, both of which promised to remove the problem of functional or "basic" literacy from the purview of Composition proper.

THE STRATEGY OF CONTAINMENT

To what extent have the circumstances that created writing centers changed over the last 30 years? Year-end reports to administrators are still written with the aim of defending the center and keeping the doors of the center open. Qualifiers are still made to faculty and administrators about plagiarism and its relation to tutoring. And then, there are the tutorials themselves that dance around the perennial question: to proofread or not to proofread. These and other elements of daily life in the writing center reflect the disciplinary instability of composition. Yet it would be wrong to say that this instability belongs to writing centers. In Althusser's terms, the instability does not originate in the infrastructure, but in a superstructure that names these and other relations of production.

To illustrate this claim, let me turn to William Yahner and William Murdick's (1991) review of early writing center history. In this review, which includes mission statements and curricular goals from over 41 institutions, the authors conclude that many early writing centers were "not primarily seen as a walk-in" facilities "but as part of a larger program in which diagnosis preceded treatment" (p. 22). Describing their own writing center at California University of Pennsylvania, they note that "under the new program, a student who failed a multiple-choice competence test for any first-year course (including the research paper course) would have to be tutored in the writing center until ready to retake the test. The effect on the writing center was disastrous: it became essentially a drill-skill factory" (p. 22). Unlike Hairston and others, however, who identify drills-and-skills with the writing centers, themselves, Yahner and Murdick describe this as a "systems-design" approach to writing program administration. The distinction is important because it begins the process of identifying the progenitors of remedial writing labs.

Betty Bamberg (1982), likewise, has described a similar model for writing program administration in which instruction takes place in two different "scenes," the lab and the classroom. In some versions, teachers refer students to the lab at their discretion. In other versions, students are required to attend the lab in order to complete a pre-arranged set of units. Writing center historian Peter Carino (1992) corroborates these accounts, noting that early writing labs were often established to improve the delivery method of the classroom. Instead of putting students through a lecture, where their individual learning problems could not be sufficiently addressed, the writing "clinic" offered individualized instruction, most often in the form of self-teaching modules, or "autotutorials," where the student could control the pace and the level of instruction. As Tori Haring-Smith, Nathaniel Hawkins, Elizabeth Morrison, Lisa Stern, and Robin Tatu (1985) point out in their overview of writing programs, "faculty and administrators" during the open admissions period, "came to believe that many students' problems went beyond the classroom" (p. 2).

This conviction, however, was not based solely on the problems of classroom methodology, although these problems were significant. As Yahner and Murdick remind us, there were racial overtones in the establishment of clinics—an emerging politics of remediation. Removing African-Americans, learning-disabled, non-native speakers, and other non-traditional students from the classroom for remediation in the clinic stigmatized them, as Carino (1992) points out, "by enclosing them in a metaphor of illness" (p. 33). If these students were indeed "healthy," if they knew the rules of standard-written English, they would not need treatment in the writing clinic.

In these ways, the clinic performed important cultural work: It helped sustain the idea of an academic community by detaining those persons in the community who were not yet eligible for membership. My point is that the clinic/lab was not compelled by current–traditional rhetoric but by a Strategy of Containment, pursued collaboratively—collegially, if you will—by English departments, administrators, writing programs, faculty, grant agencies, proponents of new technologies, and so on. As Yahner and Murdick make clear, diagnosis and treatment were not just abstractions but material practices that required administrative structures, some form of staff, and a physical location. To create a writing lab, a group of people needed to make conscious decisions to contain writing problems *elsewhere*. As well, these alliances needed to establish new methods of treating writing problems that would not disrupt the stability, continuity, and privacy of the classroom.

If writing labs provided that alternative space, it seems to me that teaching machines provided one of the instructional solutions. Thomas Barker's (1990) discussion of the 1986 MicroLab Registry illustrates the point. He notes in this survey that "drill and practice software" was used in "about twenty percent" of all computer facilities, and that of this twenty percent, nearly all were characterized as "learning assistance facilities [i.e., writing centers] whose expressed purpose is remediation"

(p. 9). He goes on to say that "these facilities are outside, or physically removed from regular writing classrooms" (p. 9), much the same way the writing centers described by Yahner and Murdick and Carino were physically removed.

In computers and composition, interest in teaching machines began in the late 1960s with mainframe computing. As early as 1968, Ellis Page had begun hand-punching student essays onto computer cards "so that the computers of the day could analyze the essays for sentence length, word length, subordination, coordination, essay length, and many other quantifiable features" (Wresch, 1984, p. 5). The results were used to sort the essays into piles—strong and weak—based on the percentage of desirable features found in a text. Like other applications of mainframe computing, these ones were expensive. They required governmental, educational, or corporate sponsors—an alliance of policy makers, professors, researchers, and funding agencies, who took interest in literacy issues. According to Paul LeBlanc, Gail Hawisher, Cynthia Selfe, and Charlie Moran (1996), the National Science Foundation (NSF), the U.S. Office of Education, and the Defense Advanced Research Projects Agency (DARPA), all "provided the substantial funding necessary to create the large, complex, and expensive first-generation CAI (computer-assisted instruction) systems" (p. 34). As well, we know that The Exxon Foundation funded Joy Reid at Colorado State University to develop WRITER'S WORKBENCH for ESL students (Kiefer & Selfe, 1983), and that IBM teamed up with faculty at Carnegie-Mellon to test the text-analysis program, EPISTLE (Neuwirth, Kaufer, & Geisler, 1984). These facts are not compelling in and of themselves. But taken together, they suggest that writing centers and computers and composition were not formed to fill the need for "basic" literacy instruction, much less to patch up a crumbling paradigm. Rather, they were formed to fulfill the needs of this alliance.

It is tempting, then, to link functional literacy with the growth of the computer industry, itself; to argue that an alliance of this nature could only be imagined in the digital age. But that would be a mistake. In 1927, long before instructional computing, S. L. Pressey imagined an instructional apparatus that would "lift from her [the teacher's] shoulders as much as possible this burden" of routine drill and practice "and make her freer for those inspirational and thought-stimulating activities which are, presumably, the real function of the teacher" (qtd. in Pagliaro, 1983, p. 75). Pressey's idea was to make mechanical devices which would save teachers time, and allow students to quiz themselves at their own pace. In his overview of computer-assisted instruction (CAI), Louis Pagliaro (1983) comments that every decade since the 1920s has seen someone like Pressey refine the idea of a teaching machine, motivated by the same promise of technical progress.

THE RHETORIC OF TECHNOCENTRISM

If it is true, then, that the impulse toward quick-fixes proceeds the computer, it should not be surprising that many early teaching machines in the writing lab were not computers but audio tapes, slides, film strips and, of course, workbooks (Nigliazzo, 1982). The computer did not create the mandate for functional literacy. It merely solidified a Rhetoric of Technocentrism that was decades in the making. As well, the computer lent an air of progress and respectability to what would have otherwise been just an embarrassing effort to contain literacy problems in a writing lab.

Consider, for example, the NCTE monograph written by Edmund J. Farrell in 1967. In it, Farrell wrote that "whether one believes the electronic revolution will have deleterious or beneficial consequences for mankind, he [sic] can not ignore it. Even those most concerned with its potentially destructive effects upon human values readily admit that the process is irreversible: one cannot halt cybernation; one may only hopefully contribute to its intelligent control" (p. 11). In this passage, Farrell emphasizes inevitable change "in" the technology, all the while reminding the reader that he or she must also change; that people not programs control the electronic revolution. "Computers," he notes, "are programmed, programs develop from conscious choices, and choices imply value systems" (p. v). Yet what is curiously absent from Farrell's discussion, are those value systems. Or rather, the discussion of values is glossed over, as I suggest below, by collapsing ideology into methodology, a move that is characteristic of technocentric arguments. Note, for example, the way in which he frames the problem that automated teaching machines were supposed to solve:

As one who supervises student teachers preparing to become secondary teachers of English, I have daily opportunity to sit in the back of classrooms and observe. During the past seven years, I have sat in over 200 classrooms and I have watched increasing numbers of students become bored with lessons which they have considered to be inane, unprofitable—in its multiple sense—and/or too slow paced. The unrest I witness differs manifestly from the clock-watching ennui I suffered as a high school student. For one thing, students frequently verbalize their dissatisfaction to the teacher, something my generation did not do. Too, their protests about what they consider to be superficial content frequently reveal an awareness of and an involvement with the issues of the times—Civil Rights, Vietnam, nonconformity—which my generation lacked. Partially, then, the following paper is a consequence of my curiosity about the ways in which electronic media are helping create students different from those in the pretelevision, pretransistor days, students who are demanding an education different at least in style and pace from that of a generation ago. The more I read about media and its effects on students, the more aware I become of how teachers will be affected by the accelerating involvement in education of electronics industries. (p. iii)

What interests me about this passage is the way technology becomes both the problem and the solution in Farrell's story of education. Students, he says, have become bored in the classroom. Yet, their boredom is not the usual student-boredom. It reflects a more serious schism between real-world issues and school-issues. This does not, however, suggest to Farrell an ideological rift between school and society. Rather, it suggests *personal* dislocation—what I visualize as fidgety students in the classroom. What Farrell finally offers as a solution, then, is a revolution in teaching methods that remains curiously aloof to the real sources of student-boredom. "Consider what might be possible in education" he asks: "Freed by the computer from dull drill, the teacher of English could spend more time in tutorials and small group discussions, engaging students about human experiences and values as they are transmitted through literature" (p. 68). What appears, then, to revolutionize the teaching of writing actually solidifies those present relations in the apparatus of functional literacy. Farrell achieves this not just by opposing Literature to Composition but by employing a Rhetoric of Technocentrism—a rhetoric that promises to make even those "dull drills" more "profitable" and effective.

According to Fred Kemp (1992), though, these promises to automate the dirty work in the teaching of writing—from grammar lessons to grading papers—fell victim to the "task-analysis fallacy, or the tendency of just about everybody in the early days of instructional computing to assume that the best computers could do was take what had always been done and do it better, faster, and cheaper" (p. 13). Proponents of the automated teaching machine, including Farrell, promised to ease the burden of teaching writing, but they did not, importantly, promise to change the meaning of writing instruction, or the relationship between functional literacy, English departments, and the university. Quite the opposite: they offered stakeholders a way to entrench those relations with an aggressively modern—and, hence, better—approach.

In short, proponents of automated instruction promised to reach out to *individuals* who, for whatever reason, could not meet the standards of the writing program. If students had problems meeting these standards, their problems must be *personal*, reflecting mal-adaptive behavior. Not surprisingly, the theoretical rationale for automation is usually derived from B.F. Skinner's work on the psychology of behavior.

In his landmark essay on behaviorism and education, Skinner (1964) argued that learning is a process of acquiring behavior, not a process of gaining knowledge. The task of the educator, he went on to say, should not be filling students' minds with information, but creating opportunities for students to change their behavior through operant conditioning. "To acquire behavior," he wrote "the student must engage in behavior. This has long been known. The principle implied in any philosophy of 'learning by doing.' But it is not enough simply to acknowledge its validity. Teaching machines provide the conditions needed to apply the principle effectively" (p. 103). What teaching machines came to represent, in other words, was a commitment to changing students' language behavior.

By "teaching machine" Skinner referred to a simple box with slide-aside panels that would provide "feedback" to the students—much like flashcards. The box allowed students to check their answers to a set of questions posed by the teacher, or printed on a ditto sheet. William Wresch (1984) pointed out in his introduction to *The Computer in Composition Studies*, that Skinner's theory of operant conditioning was behind many of the computer-based drill and practice programs developed during the mid-1960s to teach writing: "The programs taught such concepts as spelling rules, capitalization, punctuation, and grammar by taking students step by step through 'frames' in which short lessons were followed by brief tests to determine if students had mastered the spelling or grammar rule taught. (p. 5). Wresch went on to say that like Skinner, many educators felt these programs could individualize learning by providing instant, positive reinforcements in a self-paced, noncompetitive learning environment. Students would not, in this environment, have to rely on the teacher to control the pace of learning. In this limited sense, they would be free to control their own experience of the lesson.

Though Skinner did not, so far as I know, ever imagine a behaviorist writing pedagogy for college students, his work nevertheless formed the basis for such a pedagogy. Robert Zoellner (1969) laid a great deal of the ground-work in "Talk-Write: A Behavioral Pedagogy for Composition." In that monograph, he took issue with the emerging consensus in the field that writing is a way of thinking, pointing out that "our humanism may be getting in the way of our common sense, which should have told us long ago that the writing difficulties I have just described [largely related to writer's block] cannot be due entirely to 'poor preparation' or 'faulty thinking'—whatever these vague and empirically inaccessible entities may be—but rather to faulty or maladaptive behavior" (p. 271). Composition, Zoellner argued, relies too easily upon "mentalistic" abstractions that ignore, entirely, the very action of writing. Though Zoellner's essay drew many foreboding critiques of Skinnerian "conditioning," the profession did not, according to Robert Connors (1983), entirely abandon these early attempts to modify students' writing behaviors. On the contrary, the field developed some of its "most promising classroom techniques in this vein—sentence-combining, generative rhetoric, [and] imitation exercises—which essentially "languished until proven useful by conditioning techniques and carefully-controlled experimentation" (p. 17). Computers and composition likewise sustained behaviorism with sentence-combining programs (McCann, 1984), paragraphing programs (Holdstein, 1983), and thesis generating programs (Thomas & Wimett, 1984).

Advocates of teaching machines in the writing center (e.g., Kirkpatrick, 1981; Nigliazzo, 1982; Norton & Hansen, 1982; Southwell, 1984; Wittig & Bracewell, 1975), argued that the self-paced learning module did not dehumanize education but actually humanized the delivery of basic material and provided a "dignified" way for basic writers to improve their deficiencies. Students could play the tape, the film strip, or the computer program over and over again without risking public embarrassment. To many faculty and software developers, computer-assisted instruction (CAI) refined the workbook, the audio tape, and the film strip by combining all three into an interactive, presentational form. Indeed, Lynn Breininger and Stephen Portch (1983) described their CAI system as "an attractive form of workbook" (p. 358): Professor CRAM (Computer Ready Assist to Memory), used "trinkets of trivia" (p. 359) to present lively units on simple subject-verb agreement, pronoun-antecedent agreement, and other grammar exercises. Consistent with other justifications of drill and practice, the authors presented CRAM as an adjunct to writing instruction, not a replacement, and, importantly, they praised the computer for taking the grammar out of the classroom.

If, however, it was clear that the computer could contain grammar instruction, it was unclear that it could do much more than that. As Helen Schwartz (1990) poses the problem, "Will students who master the computer program be able to incorporate their learning in their own writing—or have they simply learned to guess well?" (p. 19). By contrast, when students do poorly on a computer drill, "does the fault lie with the student, the program, or the instructional setting?" (p. 19). In these questions, Schwartz frames a difficult dilemma for the pedagogy of behavior modification—one that is usually elided in discussions of CAI. Diana Cox's 1988 study provides an interesting case-in-point: Although students who used her CAI software scored higher on their weekly grammar quizzes—and thus successfully modified their behavior—it is not clear to Cox that this achievement changed their ability to compose their own texts. On this point Cox admits, "Their first paragraphs and themes were not sterling, but when I said, 'Your subject and verb don't agree' or 'That dependent adjective clause has nothing to modify,' they understood what I was saying to them in my language about their language—which is our language" (p. 163). Apparently, then, Cox's experiment was successful: Students who could not recognize subject-verb agreements before they used the software could recognize them afterwards. But as Cox, herself, points out, without invoking Skinner, this link between modified behavior and improved writing ability is murky, at best.

Consider, as further evidence, the example of HOMER, a text-analysis program that adapted Richard Lanham's *Revising Prose* for the Apple IIE. In this book, Lanham identified an "Official Style" as the enemy of good writing. As Michael Cohen and Richard Lanham (1984) described it, the official style is plagued by "a preponderance of prepositional phrases, passive verbs, noun phrases, and lengthy, shapeless sentences" (p. 84). The primary objective of HOMER, then, is the eradication of the Official Style. But Sherry Little (1987), who has tested the program, argued that the ultimate value of HOMER was not that it eradicated the Official Style, but that it problematized style: "And here I want to emphasize that HOMER paves the way to stimulating discussion, centered on the student's own writing, about the dangers of computerized text analysis and uncritical application of readability formulas in general" (p. 117). "The discussion," she says, "is lively, specific" and even "personal." Students demand to know, "computer printout in hand" why they can't use a passive construction here, or a prepositional phrase there.

Others, of course, were less sanguine about subjective responses to the medium. Consider, for example, what Kathleen Kiefer and Charles Smith (1984), had to say about WRITER'S WORKBENCH:

> Wouldn't the objectivity of a computer encourage students to adopt a more critical stance toward their writing? Wouldn't students learn more by considering surface weakness in their own work rather than in the manufactured exercises of texts and

handouts? Wouldn't a computer's objective analysis of patterns and diction and style result in more informed and more thorough stylistic revision? (p. 65)

As the authors make clear, the promise here is of increased objectivity in the feedback process. Yet as Kemp (1992) explained, this "pessimistic" side of the task-analysis fallacy assumed "that computers could only replace the agents of current processes, that computers themselves constituted no possibility of real change or major challenge to the processes themselves or to an understanding of what writing instruction is and should be" (p. 13). In this model, the faulty agent—a weak, subjective teacher—is replaced by a stronger, more objective computerized "teacher."

Naturally, as writing centers developed their own student-centered mandates to focus on actual writing tasks instead of isolated writing problems, they found the objectivity of the computer more threatening than alluring. Richard Veit's (1979) critique is representative of this attitude. In a CCCC presentation later reprinted in the *Writing Lab Newsletter*, he taunted, "the machines offer a great comfort; they're supposed to do all the work for you. Plug the students in and technology will turn them into writers" (p. 1). Veit went on to argue that basic writers do not need drills or automated feedback. They need real feedback and real experience with writing, and they need trained, caring tutors by their sides. Opposing the dubious comfort of the teaching machine to the more humane, and costly challenge of face-to-face tutoring, Veit lionized the writing center profession against technology. "Are Machines The Answer?" he asked in his title. Are writing centers based on auto-instruction? He answered his own question with a resounding "No!"

Veit's opposition proved to be well-founded, for what emerged, in place of research and scholarship on the effects of autotutorials, was just a series of testimonials and practitioner advice about programs that have proven "successful" in local contexts: pieces by Roberta Lynch (1988), and Marion Hook (1987) on using CAI with ESL students; Emil Roy (1993) and Garlie Forehand (1987) on diagnostic testing programs that inventory writing/thinking skills; and several case studies of CAI in writing centers published in 1993 (Kinkead & Harris, 1993). The average length of these articles (or article sections) is under three pages, and the average objective is to inform fellow teachers of a new program, or a successful adaptation of CAI. Authors rarely acknowledge each other's contributions, Skinner's theory, or a sense of history in the field. Evaluations of CAI—if they do appear—usually consist of a survey of student attitudes and perhaps a comparison of test scores (before/after using the software). Although innovations in CAI have emerged over the years—including tutorial programs that branch recursively to match a student's ability (Brown, 1990), and drill and practice programs that break the monotony by randomly producing "fresh" material for each lesson (Dalgish, 1987)—no major theorist in composition has re-examined Skinner's pedagogy of behaviorism, which seems to underly these programs. The silence is noteworthy.

Perhaps the lack of critical attention—here and elsewhere in the early days of computers and composition—is related to the task-analysis fallacy, itself—a strategy that precludes any theoretical or critical discussion of technology in context. What's valued most, in the task-analysis fallacy, is not critical reflection but practical expediency—a rhetoric of indisputable progress through technology. It is a rhetoric that is easily roused and re-applied in Composition, whether we are talking about word processing programs, synchronous chat programs, or hypertext writing systems.

Although writing centers eventually came to resist this rhetoric with the force of gale winds, the Strategy of Containment has limited the impact of such resistance. There was, admittedly, not much proof that teaching machines taught. But as I have suggested throughout this chapter, the lack of proof was overlooked—and still is—by political expediency. The ensuing contest to name the Real in the writing center—to establish a "center" out of a "lab"—thus began with resistance to the Rhetoric of Technocentrism. Many were understandably threatened by the promise of increased "efficiency" through technology, which replaced the weak link in the delivery system (the tutor) with a tireless, more objective "tutor." North (1979) drew the comparison in a satirical way: "In my nightmares the writing center has been made so 'efficient' that all that's left is one central, federally-funded giant Gramma Phone, out of which a computer voice dispenses chapter and verse from *The Harbrace Handbook*" (qtd. in Haring-Smith et. al., p. 6). As the satire makes clear, the imposition of technology meant the imposition of a functionalist agenda, or a reminder of its legacy: federal funds for decontextualized grammar lessons delivered through an impersonal technology.

RESISTING THE TERMS OF CONTAINMENT

Because teaching machines were often developed and maintained by a powerful network of governmental agencies, corporations, and university researchers, they seemed intractable from "the system" that many students and some faculty had come to scorn. The relentless focus on grammar and universal standards was bad enough. But the isolation one experienced with a teaching machine soon came to be symptomatic of an impersonal university that was out of touch with its students—indeed, with the culture—it served. Workers in computers and composition responded to these challenges, however, not by giving up on the idea of the teaching machine, but by transforming it, slowly, into an instrument of the composing process.

The strategy was to shift attention away from the timeless verities of style and grammar—those concerns of the state or the system—and to refocus that attention on the contingencies of individual creativity. The aim, more specifically, was to jump start the thinking process with automated dialogue programs. In her essay on computerized pre-writing, Nold (1975) made it clear what was at stake: "if the computer teaching programs developed so far are unimaginative and dull, the author, not the computer, must take responsibility" (p. 270). Not one to shirk responsibility, Nold went on to describe three programs that she created at Stanford University:

one designed for writing poetry, another for writing persuasive essays, and the last for exploring logical fallacies.

Of course, proponents of these programs were not alone in their struggles to jump start the student's thinking process. In the first dissertation on computerized pre-writing, Hugh Burns (1979) cited the work of Lee Odell, Kenneth Pike, Richard Young, Janice Lauer, Gordon Rhomann, and others who, without computers, had situated the idea of pre-writing within rhetoric and developmental, cognitive psychology. As Burns made clear citing Frank D'Angelo, "invention always seems to take place within a system" (p. 7), and that system, however embedded in the writer's mind, is not entirely absent from view. "Granted," Burns went on to say, "a teacher cannot teach insight" but he or she can "prompt students to make discoveries" by providing "systematic strategies or procedures" (p. 5). The pedagogical idea behind these programs, Nold recognized, was not to get computers to "do things" for students but to get students to do things for themselves. The following transcript, taken from Burns' dissertation, illustrates the process. The student's responses have been boldfaced.

> During this exploration process, you will be asked to clarify the purpose of your paper on the fear of death. So how would you briefly describe the purpose of your paper by completing this statement: The purpose of this paper is to . . .
> **Examine the fear of death people have, where we get those fears, and how we may reduce those fears.**
> Fine, Walt, you and I will talk again about your purpose. Relax now, Walt, and enjoy this brainstorming session. What objects do you associate with the fear of death? How might they be included in your theme?
> **Fear of the unknown, cessation of life, fear of causing pain to our loved ones.**
> That's the idea, Walt. Give me some more info now.
> **Pain is another fear causer, knowing we have to die does not relieve the pain/fear of dying.**
> Super, Walt! Anything else? (You can add more info, ask a question, or give a command—whatever you wish.)
> **How does euthanasia, mercy killing, suicide, murder, and accidental death add to our fears?**
> I could say that that's for me to know and you to find out. Seriously, I cannot pretend to knowhow, but you should keep exploring for an answer. (qtd. in Kellog, 1989, p. 73)

When Walt asks that last question beginning with "How," the computer responds with its stock answer to content questions <I cannot pretend to know how> throwing the ball back in the student's court. Helen Schwartz has argued that after a series of responses like this one, students eventually "realize they cannot get answers from the computer. They soon revel in the fact that they are doing the thinking, not the machine" (qtd. in Kemp, 1987, p. 38). Thus, by emphasizing the writer's responsibility to think for him or herself, pre-writing proponents made a decisive break from functionalism, but not necessarily from the task-analysis fallacy.

As it was with automated feedback or automated grammar instruction, the goal here was to automate some part of the teaching process, in this case, pre-draft thinking. Pre-writing software not only benefited the student struggling to invent ideas, it benefited the teacher who wanted to save on conference time. Rather than sit with students and ask them what they want to write about, the teacher could direct students to the appropriate program. Defenders of these programs are quick to point out that computerized tutors are "tireless" and "infinitely patient," and in many ways the idealized tutors (Arms, 1983; Burns, 1979; Schwartz, 1984). Conferences with these "tutors," according to Ronald Kellog (1989), not only help students invent ideas but help them handle the emotional and cognitive "overload" associated with writing. An invention program, Kellog said, could become a surrogate therapist or a personal trainer who helps the writer "funnel" his attention on the task at hand. James Strickland (1985) and Raymond and Dawn Rodrigues (1984) added that the ultimate pre-writing environment would not only offer the student a choice amongst programs, but a choice amongst cognitive levels and thinking "styles." Like a "Lifecycle" machine, any given program could be modulated, or tailored to fit a writer's affective and cognitive needs, becoming a constant companion in the writing process—what Burns (1984) described as "a kind of mental fitness center" (p. 16).

As it turned out, there were problems with these assumptions. Elizabeth Klem and Charles Moran (1991) have noted, for example, that early pre-writing programs were not even integrated with word processors. The implicit signal this sent to the writer was that generating ideas came before writing, not during writing. Strickland (1986) also found that although students could generate many ideas with structured heuristic programs, they in fact used relatively few of these ideas in their own writing. Burns, himself, had worried about "overstimulating" the student during the invention stage. Strickland's study not only confirmed that fear but offered another caveat. According to his study, students who used the less structured pre-writing program, which was based on Elbow's (1973) freewriting method, tended to find more ideas that they actually wanted to pursue in their papers. This study, it seems, highlighted the obvious: while the computers and composition was trying to rescue the teaching machine by engineering the thinking process, the computer had already offered an interface that was far more provocative: the blank screen and video text.

Word processing programs soon earned the position of honor in the field, then, by becoming a "pure" interface with the mind. Where pre-writing programs had assumed that deep structure could be generalized into what Burns (1979) called "non-data conditioned heuristics," (p. 8) word processing assumed that flexible video text could, by itself, help writers find their own structure. It seems that many hopes were pinned on word processing. As Maurice Scharton and Janice Neuleib (1990) summarized in a special issue of *The Writing Center Journal* devoted to computing, "the most valuable contribution the computer could make to writing [centers] is the freedom to compose and revise at will" (p. 50). When writers see their words "dancing around the screen," Stephen Marcus added (1984), they suddenly get a much different sense of their commitment to the "final" copy. On screen, words are no longer "carved in stone" (p. 122). Words are flexible, ephemeral, and intimately composed. Unlike the typewriter, which forced writers to either commit to their composing decisions or rip up the page in frustration, word processing technologies allowed writers to separate the act of composing from the act of printing. This reprieve from the printed record, gave writers a new freedom to "say anything" that was much celebrated, not just in Composition Studies, but throughout higher education and beyond. With word processing programs, the computer was no longer an artificial tutor in the center, but a writer's tool. Robert Levin (1984) went so far as to argue that with word processing, a writing center director could "alter the character of the center":

> To the extent that the writing center is traditionally and predominantly used by weaker English students, it has the character of a remedial zone. When this character is pronounced, the instruction is stigmatized, and the center has a depressed ambiance. Where this pattern prevails, word processing instruction, and the students who aggressively seek it out, can offer relief. Soon after CAW [computer-assisted writing] is introduced, a new breed of students—bright, energetic, curious about or already expert on the computer, and eager to share computer stories—begins to appear at the center, which becomes a place not only for remediation but also a place for experimentation and high-level intellectual activity and a think tank for the best and brightest students. The resultant mix of remedial and high-caliber students can be almost utopian in both its social and academic aspects. (p. 47)

By luring "the best and brightest" into the "remedial zone" for word processing, Levin argued that a writing center director could re-define the center as a space for "intellectual activity." Researchers in computers and composition, however, took it much further than that. Colette Daiute (1983), for example, claimed that "the interactiveness of the text editor [can] stimulate a writer to take a reader's point of view" (p. 134) not only by making writing physically easier, thus allowing her to concentrate better, but by extending a writer's memory capacity. In this way, the computer could allegedly facilitate the production of what Linda Flower (1979) called "reader-based prose." The assumption, however reasonable, ultimately suggested more faith in technology than in students, as it positioned students passively: the objects of word processing programs. The hypothesis was nevertheless tested in a bevy of new studies on word processing. Because many of these studies did not examine writers writing, but only the finished products, researchers were forced into the experimentalist mode of isolating variables (pen-and-paper vs. word processor), testing those variables in controlled situations, and somehow gleaning from the experiment how "the technology" affected the look of the final product. Had the research been conclusive, there would perhaps be a different story to tell. But as Gail Hawisher (1987) explains, the results were anything but conclusive.

Last year, in the November 1986 issue of *Computers and Composition*, I reviewed 24 studies conducted in word processing since 1981 and concluded that, for the most part, results were varied and conflicting. Some studies reported increased revision and improved quality (e.g., Daiute, 1986; Womble, 1985) whereas others noted increased revision and no improvement in quality (e.g., Gould, 1981; Collier, 1983; Daiute, 1984, 1985; Duling, 1985). Still others reported that neither the quality of the revision nor the success of the writing improved significantly when students produced texts with word processing (e.g., Hawisher, 1987). Since last year, 16 additional studies have appeared in professional journals or *Dissertation Abstracts International* (DAI) and, if we examine the two variables of revision and quality, contradictory results continue to emerge. (p. 7)

If researchers could not determine that word processing increased a student's revising activity and thus the quality of the text, what could they determine? What *did* word processing do to texts? The results are, in many ways, embarrassing. According to Hawisher, "an increased number of words appears to be the most agreed upon finding" (p. 11). "Teachers might well question what qualitative difference 30 or so more words possibly makes in student writing" (p. 17). A less quantifiable but more solid claim, across the 16 studies she reviewed in 1987 and the 24 she reviewed in 1986, was that students seemed to like word processing. Surely positive attitudes counted for something.

THE ETHIC OF INTERVENTION

Against this backdrop of technocentrism, writing centers proponents such as Veit argued forcefully that with or without computers, the main challenge in writing instruction is to intervene in and eventually alter the student's process of writing. Ann Moseley (1984), for example, who rejected her own "factory model" of the writing lab in favor of a "workshop" approach, discovered that "overworked tutors, like job foremen" dispensing materials to students, cannot hope to address the "individual student and his or her writing process" (p. 33). Although methodologies and rationales vary, interventionists are generally committed, as Harris (1990) points out, "to taking the student out of the group and looking at her as an individual, as a person with all her uniqueness" (p. 19). North (1984) draws the comparison between this interventionist model and its functionalist "other" this way: "Whereas in the 'old' center instruction tends to take place after or apart from writing, and tends to focus on the correction of textual problems, in the 'new' center the teaching takes place as much as possible during writing, during the activity being learned, and tends to focus on the activity itself" (p. 439). Judith Summerfield (1988) points out that this shift in sensibility inevitably decentered the role of the teacher:

What we began to recognize, particularly through the one-to-one encounter in tutoring was that we are all different. There are different ways of composing, of reading, of experiencing the world. Different minds, different experiences. Those of us who came to tutoring from teaching quickly realized that we could no longer construe our students as a homogenous blob. (p. 5)

This recognition of difference soon characterized tutorials as highly individualized encounters. Working one-to-one allowed—even demanded—that instruction be tailor-made, not mass produced. The writing tutor became an auditor, beginning and ending the session with the student's agenda. As Daniel T. Lochman (1986) explains:

In the one-to-one discussion that occurs at most writing centers, students have an immediate, easily accessible audience, one prepared to respond without external rewards such as grades but with genuine, human responses to students' attempts at communication. At their best, writing centers allow students, especially basic writers, the opportunity to play with language—often for the first time in an educational setting. (p. 16)

Yet the dynamics of this interaction—the "play with language"— are predicated on the idea that the writer is an individual composer moving through stages or experiences in the composing process. This can readily be seen in the theories of intervention that are based on generalized models of the composing process. These theories posit an individual writer who is essentially stuck or blocked at one stage or another in the composing process, who comes to the writing center to get "un-stuck," as it were, or back on the track. One-to-one instruction in the composing process finally becomes a problem of location: where is the student in this process?

To navigate composing locations, or to find the writer in the process, North (1982) developed a diagnostic tool called "The Composing Profile," with two components: a survey on "prerequisite skills, history, attitudes, and study skills" related to writing, and a "composing chart"—with textual features listed vertically and recursive stages of the writing process listed horizontally—the latter, which the tutor used to diagnose symptoms "that cause difficulty" in the text (p. 48). North presented the composing profile as a systematic approach to diagnosis, in which the tutor helped the writer re-conceive her approach to the writing task. With this tool, the tutor might then intervene in that writer's process, offering diagnosis, instruction, and support at any number of composing locations—exploration, editing, and so on—variously defined in relation to models of the composing process and the student's unique interpretation of those models. There is, admittedly, a tension here between the student's unique process and the more generalized models of the composing process. Thus, North qualifies his version of process, claiming first that writing is a recursive process, not a linear one (as the naming of "stages" would indicate) and that these models of the composing process are "provisional" rather than definitive—a heuristic for diagnosis, not a means of rigidly sorting students.

However, any foray into process immediately, though perhaps unwittingly, blurs the line between the writer and his writing, making it difficult to limit the scope of an intervention: a tutor does not just help the writer write but to think. To find out where the student is located involves layers of interpretation not just in relation to some model of the composing process, but to thinking processes, and the beliefs or commitments that accompany those processes. Lou Kelly, for example, described the conference as a place "where [students] can hear their writing as the voice of the unique human being each of them is and is becoming" (p. 19). The writing, in this sense, becomes a window into the mind's activity, and tutors who intervene are implicitly—or in some cases, explicitly—asked to peer through this window.

Phyllis Lassner (1984) described this scene beyond the window in a developmental context, locating the tutorial within James Britton's discourse theory and D.W. Winnicott's psychoanalytic theory. In Britton's discourse theory, the teacher must first nurture writing "close to the self" by encouraging the student to take risks without fear of judgment and, only after mutual trust has been established, encourage the student to break away from the expressive self, and address a more distant audience in standard-written English. In Winnicott's "maturational process," a similar sequence takes place, where the "mother" encourages the child's development by establishing an empathetic bond and then weans the child away from that relationship, encouraging psychological independence. In both Britton's discourse theory and Winnicott's psychoanalytic theory, the student (and the child) develop a strong emotional bond with the teacher (and the mother) before achieving independence.

Perhaps the most well-known manifesto in the interventionist literature is Stephen North's (1984), "The Idea of the Writing Center." In it, North made "a declaration of independence" from those progenitors of the early writing lab, advocating, instead, a "pedagogy of direct intervention" into the student's writing process. The challenge, in other words, was to hail the writer differently, not as an organism with maladaptive behaviors, but as an autonomous thinker, capable of making decisions about her own learning." What we want to do in a writing center," North (1984) wrote, "is fit into—observe and participate in—this ordinarily solo ritual of writing" (p. 439). This ritual, he also says, is not easily explained by versions of "the" writing process. "The version we want can only be found, in as yet unarticulated form, in the writer we are working with" (p. 438).

Much like the move toward pre-writing dialogue programs and word processing programs in computers and composition, this move signaled a break with the apparatus of functional literacy insofar as the student was granted a humanistic form of agency that transcended his or her external behavior. Other attempts to theorize this agency came from the philosophy of language. In their discussion of a talk-aloud writing protocol, Knoblauch and Brannon (1984) argue that since meaning is created organically by students, through the very act of writing, tutors should be cautious of imposing an "Ideal Text" over the student's developing text, lest they risk interfering with the student's natural development of language abilities. This blurring of the writer within the seamless web of language sometimes goes even further, and writing becomes akin to living, or an ethic for living, as when Warnock and

Warnock (1984) encourage students to "'rewrite' themselves and their worlds" (p. 16). In their argument for a "liberatory" writing center, Warnock and Warnock make use of Suzanne Langer, Kenneth Burke, and Ernst Cassirier, positing "language as symbolic action" (p. 18), a primal medium for self-creation. They reject the "survival skills" rationale for writing centers, arguing instead that writing centers can—and should—be more ambitious: In short, liberatory centers should create critical consciousness, where "students learn the practical skills of learning to live in the face of determinate and indeterminate meaning" (p. 16). Students, in other words, need to see changes in their writing as changes in their lives: Revising the page means revising those ways of thinking that are inhibiting one's life.

In many ways, these theoretical overlapping rationales from composition theory, psychoanalytic theory, and the philosophy of language only clarify the Ethic of Intervention. When intervention works, it deliberately blurs the line between the writer and his or her writing. The writer reveals what went into the writing—how it was made, what it represents—and the writing reveals, however obliquely, who or what the writer is—or is becoming. As North (1984) generalizes, "we look beyond or through that particular project, that particular text, and see it as an occasion for addressing *our* primary concern, the process by which it is produced" (p. 438).

That tutors can, or should, intervene in a students' writing is accepted as a given in the literature on conferencing. There is, quite frankly, a bootstrapping mentality at work: however collaborative or mutual a conference may be, its aim is to show the writer not only how to generate material—to shape it and re-write it—but to inhabit it, to grow "in" it, to pull oneself up through it. Rudolph Almasy (1982) summarizes, "as lab instructor and student consistently review the written product together, they rehearse what the student—we hope—will eventually do alone" (p. 18). Yet Lassner (1984) adds that "the student cannot become autonomous unless the instructor is ready to let go" (p. 26). Intervening then becomes a negotiation of authority, even without a physical draft to work on. Seen this way, "the paper" becomes

an illusion because although it belongs to the student, the process of creation is nurtured by the instructor. It belongs, in fact, somewhere between them as a transitional object, facilitating both dependence on the instructor and independence through communication. As we negotiate the potential paper between us, the student and I must accept its paradoxical position, learning as well, a critical way of understanding irresolution, ambiguity—in short process. (p. 28)

Yet the negotiation of authority and its treatment in the interventionist literature, does not always proceed as neatly as Lassner suggests. In "The Politics of Writing Conferences," Jane Melnick (1984) shows that this "paradoxical position" of the paper, neither entirely the student's nor the tutor's, can create dysfunctional conversations where both sides assert control, but fail to yield it. In one of three conferences Melnick analyzes, this crisis of authority actually stalemated communication between herself and her student. The student, "Frederika, tall, pale, dressed with drama and fastidiousness" (p. 16) makes an argument against abortion by quoting long passages from the Bible, and Melnick, who "found the argument from predestination very difficult" (p. 18) nevertheless asks her to imagine different rhetorical contexts for the argument. Frederika, however, resists this idea, responding "in a resigned tone" and showing Melnick through this tone of voice and behavior that "only complete agreement with not only her beliefs, but her rhetorical approach to them would free her from this feeling" of resistance (p. 19).

Unlike the other tutorials Melnick analyzes, this one is judged unsuccessful, but not surprisingly because of the ethical dispute over abortion, but because the conversation fails to empower Frederika. Naturally, the "successful" tutorials worked because Melnick was able to empower her students. In her discussion of one of the other tutorials she comments, "Once I had, in effect, given [the student] permission to use her own mind to figure out writing problems, [she] seemed to enter a whole new world; a world where she realized she had authority over her own meaning" (p. 16). Yet Frederika, who ironically already has authority over her own meaning and sustains that authority through resistance of Melnick, stymies the idea of "successful" intervention: Melnick cannot intervene because she cannot negotiate a place in Frederika's textual world. This irony, however, does not complicate Melnick's conclusion: "By using our authority decisively, we are not necessarily taking control away from students; if we can clarify both in our actions and our words that our authority is clear but limited, students can experience the reality that they must and can take on basic authority—and responsibility—for their writing" (p. 20).

One of the main stumbling points in the interventionist model, then, is this alleged neutrality, or objectivity of the tutor, who "gives" authority to students. Indeed, the very idea of intervention suggests an impartial but enthusiastic counselor patiently drawing the client out. Yet as Melnick makes clear, nonjudgmental listening in the tradition of Carl Rogers is not always possible. In "Subjectivity in the Tutorial Session: How Far Can We Go?," Stacey Freed (1989) frames the dilemma as an ethical issue. Though she admits "we must always go back to the task at hand, the writing," she also insists that we "be prepared to question students on their beliefs, to check them on the validity of their arguments" (p. 42). But the problem with this stance, as Freed seems to recognize, is the risk of losing the student's trust, especially if the tutor's questions create dissensus: in Melnick's tutorial with Frederika, any suggestion she made became a directive or a threat to Frederika's autonomy. And the problem is not isolated to Freed or Melnick. In an informal survey of tutors, Freed "found most tutors had the urge to enter discussion/debate with their students, but saw the writing itself as the first priority" (p. 40). What about that paper "that goes against one's fundamental beliefs?," Freed asks. "Do we ignore ethical issues and "focus on 'higher-order concerns' of structure? Do we ask this person to back up his argument with examples?" (p. 39). Do we intervene or interfere?

CONSTRUING NEW RELATIONS

It is, admittedly, tempting to downplay these problems and instead draw the following conclusion: After fighting off functionalism, the writing center emerged—bruised, perhaps, but still standing and strong—the victor with a victor's mandate: "to produce," in North's (1984) words, "better writers, not better writing" (p. 438). Yet the problem with this kind of conclusion, as North (1994) more recently pointed out, is that it tends to romanticize the practice of conferencing. It assumes, rather narrowly, that battles have been fought and largely won—if not materially, through better working conditions, then at least morally: writing centers become, in North's original formulation from the 1984 essay, "centers of consciousness" about writing in the college. Yet what has been won is not so much the moral high ground but a dubious "right" to intervene in the writer's process, and a tenuous construction of writerly agency in the student body. North illustrates the dilemma of this situation below.

> Regardless of the commitment by a writing center staff to reforming the larger institution, the tendency seems not for the center to become the locus of any larger consciousness. On the contrary, there is a very strong tendency for it to become the place whose existence serves simultaneously to locate a wrong-ness (in this case, illiteracy, variously conceived) *in* a set of persons (and in that sense to constitute language differences *as* a wrong-ness); to absolve the institution from further consideration of such persons, in that they have now been named ('basic,' 'remedial,' 'developmental') and 'taken care of'; and, not incidentally, to thereby insulate the institution from any danger to its own configuration the differences such persons are now said to embody might otherwise pose. In short—and to put it in the most sinister terms—this particular romanticization of the writing center's institutional potential may actually mask its complicity in what Elspeth Stuckey has called the violence of literacy. (p. 15)

Though most writing centers would like to imagine themselves outside of these politics, the problem is, in North's view, systemic. By isolating problematic students from the curricular flow of things, writing centers can become just as vulnerable as the students they serve. By insisting that their ideal teaching situation (one-on-one with the student) is actually created through this isolation from the academic community, writing centers often perpetuate their own vulnerability as mere support services. They become scapegoats for problems that, in fact, belong to the institution. To intervene at the curricular, pedagogical, and technological levels, writing centers need not give up their perceived independence or their student-centered mandate, at least not absolutely. But they should—and we should—move beyond what I see as an entrenched and, in many ways, defensive isolationism.

Another liability that we incur from a rigid defense of Intervention, is a set of institutional roles for the writer and the tutor that, in some ways, preclude the construction of other, electronic roles. Why, for example, are Kathy Vasile and Nick

Ghizzone (1992) compelled to begin their essay on "Computer-Integrated Tutoring" with this qualification?: "The introduction of computers into the Brookdale Community College Writing Lab did not mean that human tutors were replaced by electronic ones" (p. 17). Even though their article has nothing to do with autotutorials, they feel compelled to acknowledge and then discount the legacy before they can begin. Consider, as well, the manner in which Joyce Kinkead positions the email tutor in the writing center. Although she describes email as "intrinsically motivating" (1987), she also worries that email could be perceived by budget-conscious administrators as a replacement for the more expensive practice of face-to-face tutoring. "Our response" to this threat, writes Kinkead (1988), should be that "while electronic tutoring provides supplementary tutoring and combats the problems of time and distance for students needing tutorial help, such tutoring does not equal the value of dialogue in a face-to-face (f2f) conference" (p. 5). These "supplements," in other words, are certainly valuable but they should never be confused with "real" tutoring.

The problem with this formulation is not the skeptical attitude toward budget-conscious administrators. That, at least, is understandable. Likewise, I am not troubled by Kinkead's defense of the face-to-face (f2f) conference. It is, after all, a compelling scene of teaching. No, what bothers me is the oppositional logic—the notion that email tutoring is really just a bad version or a non-version of real tutoring. The opposition to computers, of course, is understandable but also misplaced, for what it really indicates is a resistance to the apparatus of functional literacy. Other forms of resistance to this apparatus, including the Ethic of Intervention and the pre-writing movement in computers and composition, have not been futile. But neither have they been impenetrable to the ongoing politics of technocentrism and containment.

As I've suggested, writing centers and computers and composition are not self-contained entities anymore than Composition is a self-contained discipline or literacy is a self-contained concept. All are enmeshed in a much larger drama about the function of general education in professional culture, the identity of the university, and the role of writing in the academic community. If Russell is right in suggesting that this "community" is no more connected by transportable writing skills than transportable math skills, then we ought to reconsider the ways both fields are implicated in the idea of community. As Joseph Harris (1989) suggests, students do not so much confront a single interpretive community or even a speech community when they come to college, but "several continuous and conflicting discourses . . . . of home, school, work, the media, and the like—to which they already belong" (p. 275). The task of the writing teacher is not to initiate students into a single community but to help students find ways to sort through those discourses that compete for their attention.

Though Harris does not make reference to writing centers or computers in his article, I believe electronic writing centers can become places to do the kind of work that he suggests we do, but only if writing centers are willing to look beyond the roles that they have so lovingly constructed for the tutor and the writer; only if others in Composition are willing to invest resources in writing center activities that are not premised, nostalgically, upon the resurrection of community. Likewise, if writing centers go on to assume that the only reason to use computers in the tutorial is to replicate what we already do—to do it faster, better, and cheaper—we will fall victim, again, to the task-analysis fallacy, precluding the possibility of changing what we do or how we are perceived. The practice of email "tutoring" and the theory of dialogic literacy, as I will suggest in the next two chapters, cannot safeguard writing centers from future hails in the ISA of literacy, but they can provide a space for informed resistance.

2

Email "Tutoring" and Dialogic Literacy

The biggest challenge teachers face today in connection with computers is not that of using technology—we are already doing so—but rather that of using technology to make a real difference in our classrooms. We can sit back and let computers be introduced into our programs in quiet ways that will change little: our students will sit in isolated study carrels doing grammar drill-and-practice programs or will labor alone with word-processing programs to complete their papers. . . . Or we can draw on the revolutionary potential of computer technology to create non-traditional forums that allow students the opportunity to reexamine the authoritarian values of the classroom, to resist their socialization into a narrowly conceived form of academic discourse, to learn from the clash of discourses, to learn through engaging discourse.
— (Cooper & Selfe, 1990, p. 867)

In the last chapter, I argued that, to a large extent, writing centers and computers and composition have made plausible the idea of a process revolution by containing functional literacy within their laboratory spaces. So long as behavior modification did not take up class time, so long as "slow" students or those with dialects or those who spoke English as a second language could be identified and treated, so long as the "other" could be accommodated outside the classroom—in those study carrels, perhaps, that Cooper and Selfe refer to—functional literacy could be encouraged

27

and, at the same time, renounced by the discipline as current–traditional. Shabby accommodations in this House of Lore, however, soon led both fields to contest the ways that they had been hailed. Students, they argued, are not organisms with faulty language behaviors. They are human beings with the will power and the desire to make meaning. When a human being finds expression difficult he or she does not need a series of grammar drills but a conversation with another human being.

Although this interventionist platform for tutoring has succeeded in humanizing the writing center, it is not clear that it has done much more than that. If intervention does, in fact, relieve some of the tensions that students experience while writing in the university, it does not necessarily change the conditions that created those tensions: poorly constructed writing assignments, uninspired teaching, condescending textbooks, and confusing, or mean-spirited, end-comments from professors. "This isn't to be cynical about the possibilities for 'genuine' or 'deep' engagement," says North (1994). "It is rather to contextualize such notions, to (re)situate them in the school culture" (p. 11). That culture, as I have already suggested, can be rather unforgiving; so much so that even the "good" writers who come to the center remain convinced that they have serious deficiencies in their writing.

We know from the history with teaching machines and, more generally, from the Rhetoric of Technocentrism, that computers have been used to entrench the Strategy of Containment. But we also know from pioneering figures such as Ellen Nold and Hugh Burns, that computers do not create programs that sustain the idea of functional literacy. People do. So, while technology cannot change the meaning of literacy, people can, as Eric Crump (1995) says, become technoprovocateurs of literacy, if they take a critical approach to instructional computing, or tap into the revolutionary potential that Cooper and Selfe describe. In this chapter, then, I will argue that a Bakhtinian approach to email "tutoring" is, in fact, one way of becoming a technoprovocateur; one way of defining a new mandate for the writing center that cuts against the Strategy of Containment and the Rhetoric of Technocentrism.

This form of interaction, I will argue, bears less resemblance to traditional "tutoring" and more resemblance to collaborative writing. The relationship is not so much tutor to student but writer to writer. In this way, email "tutoring" exploits what Marilyn Cooper (1994) describes, in her discussion of dialogic learning, as "the pressure of infinite semiosis [or] the always available possibility that the utterance could be understood differently" (p. 536). To use email as a site for "infinite semiosis" is to deny the assumption that writing centers exist only to solve functional problems in student writing. A pedagogy of infinite semiosis implies that "problems" are always the sponsor of further discourse, places to begin a conversation, not objects of diagnosis. Email "tutoring" works, in other words, when it creates a new infrastructure of computing and conferencing in the ISA of literacy. Before I get to my transcripts of the email sessions, however, I would like to take stock of the face-to-face (f2f) conference, not so much as a pedagogy, or as an Ethic of Intervention, but as a methodology.

FACE-WORK IN THE WRITING CENTER

John Trimbur (1987) has already suggested that peer tutoring represents a contradiction in terms because it places the tutor in a liminal role, half-way between the status of students and the status of teachers. What Trimbur draws attention to is the performative nature of tutoring, where tutors must assume different roles throughout the conference. I would take it one step further and argue that during the writing conference, both the tutor and the student must enter into a temporal sequence of negotiation; that this process, like any interaction ritual, is activated by what Erving Goffman (1967) calls co-presence. A closer analysis of these dynamics may shed some light on the dynamics of online tutoring.

Within the time-bound struggle to establish the session as a session—why are we here? what are trying to accomplish?—the tutor and the student construct each other, as Erving Goffman (1967) says, ritualistically: Each person emits a "line," receives feedback on the line, and uses that feedback to adjust his or her behavior according to the other person's expectations or needs. The object is to maintain an expressive order consistent with one's sense of self and institutional possibility. Writing centers are no different, in this sense, than the villages or hospitals that Goffman studied. Each place allows a limited range of conversational moves, while disallowing others.

To Goffman, then, the study of face-work is not the study of individuals but the study of the "behavioral order found in all peopled places" (p. 2). The materials, he notes, "are glances, gestures, positioning, and verbal statements that people continuously feed into the situation, whether intended or not" (p. 1). Although Goffman always holds out the possibility for changing the behavioral order, for example, through the cultivation of an underlife (1961), he is just as likely or more likely to see the social arena as one that compels an individual to wear a "tragic mask" (1959, p. 57). In *Interaction Ritual* (1967) he notes the fragile relation between our masks and our selves:

> In any case, while his social face can be his most personal possession and the center of his security and pleasure, it is only on loan to him from society; it will be withdrawn unless he conducts himself in a way that is worthy of it. Approved attributes and their relation to face make of every man his own jailer; this is a fundamental social constraint even though each man may like his cell. (p. 10)

One gets the sense, while reading Goffman, that someone is always about to lose face, gain face, or in other ways be compromised by a trenchant glance, an inappropriate compliment, or a poorly executed departure.

What Melnick and her student Frederika seem to discover, in that session that I discussed in Chapter One, is that their lines are not helping, but rather hindering, face work. Neither one is willing to become what the other one wants her to become, hence each one senses a threat to their social face. Melnick, it seems, is unwilling to be complicit in Frederika's conservative argument about abortion, and Frederika is unwilling to reconsider the rhetoric of her argument, or, so it seems, to take any criticism at all. Having failed to establish the conditions for mutual reinforcement, both find it difficult to imagine alternatives. Frederika seems unwilling to think differently about her expectations of the tutor, just as Melnick seems unwilling to reconsider what it means to empower the student. Of course, the stalemate is understandable. As Goffman (1959) reminds us, there are significant risks involved in face work:

> The individual's initial projection commits him to what he is proposing to be and requires him to drop all pretenses of being other things. As the interaction among the participants progresses, additions and modifications will of course occur, but it is essential that these later developments be related without contradiction to, and even built up from, the initial positions taken by the several participants. (pp. 10–11)

What Goffman draws attention to here is the latent conservatism of face work: When a person commits to a certain line of behavior, that line can be difficult to reverse. The price of reversal could be the loss of face. And here, it is important to read loss in two ways, as a loss of the expressive order and a loss of ideological common ground.

To Goffman, these moments when things break down are interesting only insofar as they set into motion a corrective process that re-establishes—or fails to re-establish—everyone's faces. It seems natural, here, to read "face" as "self;" to construe the corrective process as a self-creating, self-sustaining process. But to Goffman, it is not clear that this is really the case. "It may not even be necessary," he writes in *The Presentation of Self in Everyday Life* (1959), "to decide which is more real, the fostered impression or the one the performer attempts to prevent the audience from receiving" (p. 66). The impressions are really all that we have. We may work frantically to sustain those impressions, but the relation between that work and our "selves" is unclear, or at least, it is about as clear as the relation between an actor's character and an actor's self, or the author's hero and the author's self. There is a relation, but not a direct one—not one that is perceptible to another in any definitive way.

Goffman's work is suggestive, in this context, because it complicates our understanding of pure intervention. I bring it up not to discredit the practice of working with students face-to-face—anymore than I brought up word processing research to discredit the instructional value of word processing—but to draw attention to the methodological limitations. The assumption, here, is that tutoring offers a window into the writer's mind. Goffman helps us to understand, however, that students and tutors are not always what they seem; that convincing performances "could still have been managed" or in other ways compromised by alternative needs to save face. I am not suggesting that all f2f sessions are methodologically deceptive. But, as Goffman points out, "to be a given kind of person" is to "sustain the standards of conduct" in the behavioral order. "Status," he notes, "is not a material thing, to be possessed and then displayed" but something that must be "enacted and portrayed" (1959, pp. 71–75). The issue, finally, is not whether a performance is true or false, but "whether or not the performer is authorized to give the performance in question" (p. 59). To be authorized to perform in the writing center, one needs much more than training or rehearsal but a credible "face" as a writer or a tutor.

FACE-WORK WITHOUT FACES

When I first began tutoring students that I could not see, I was drawn to Goffman's work, in part, because I wanted to assure myself that, despite the relative anonymity of email conferencing, there really was a tutorial process. Yet if an online writing conference was not held together by face-work, then what held it together? Are email tutors still participant-observers in the student's writing process? If so, what are they participating in? What are they observing? Also, when students correspond with a tutor online, is this correspondence considered a part of their composing process? If so, why? What is the difference between the writer of the paper and the writer of the email?

As critical theorist Andrew Feenberg (1989) points out, in an online environment, individuals have the impression—real or perceived—that they can control their presentation of self in ways that are not possible face to face: A sentence written in haste can be deleted before being broadcast to the group. No such parallel exists in face-to-face communication. (You can't take back what you've uttered aloud.) Yet this newfound power to "control" the presentation of oneself is misleading, because it appears to extend the writer's power to control social interaction. By writing oneself instead of speaking oneself, one gains crucial time to consider and reconsider one's image of self before making a move in the interaction ritual. "By increasing the individuals' control of image," says Feenberg, "while diminishing the risk of embarrassment, computer talk alters the sociological ratio of the two dimensions of selfhood and opens up a new social space" (p. 25).

Of course, the advantage that Feenberg highlights could also be construed as a disadvantage for both tutors and writers who are unable or unwilling to "control" their presentation of self in writing. What I see in email tutoring, however, is not so much a lack of social context cues as an abundance of dialogic cues, or potential "images" of the self that are provocative to explore. The very activity of writing, which is often associated with privacy and authorial privilege in the center (Never write on the student's text! Never hold the pen during the conference!) becomes with email a public act where both parties hold keyboards. Co-presence is not given. It must be made.

The email tutorials that I discuss in this book were all conducted at SUNY-Albany (Albany, NY) between 1992–1995 as part of a pilot project in the University Writing Center. The mission of The University Writing Center, at that time under the direction of Lil Brannon, was to support students' efforts at writing across the curriculum. SUNY-Albany is a large state university and, hence, the writing center serves many students from a variety of disciplines, primarily in the humanities and the social sciences. Graduate and undergraduate tutors were drawn, almost exclusively, from the English department. The writing center supported the email tutoring project by including it in its weekly meeting as a topic for discussion and by encouraging all students and tutors to experiment with email sessions.

As the coordinator of this project, I encouraged undergraduate and graduate students to send their texts as email messages to an account named WRITING, which we set up on the university's VAX computer. Advertisements for the service and instructions for using it were posted electronically and physically around campus. Students were initially promised instant turn-around if they made contact with WRITING during posted hours. Later, I dropped the posted hours and promised a two day turn-around. In practice, students often received feedback much sooner.

Since most of the writing center computers, at that time, did not have email, students and tutors who participated in the project would usually send and receive messages from campus computer labs and from their homes, carrying on a correspondence with each other for two or three days. WRITING received, on average, about five requests for assistance per week. The messages were read, primarily, by graduate student teaching-assistants, including myself, who were enrolled in SUNY's English Department. The four tutors, who all had previous experience in the writing center, volunteered approximately five hours a week. As a group, we occasionally met to discuss the theory and practice of email tutoring. But generally, we did not work in the same space at the same time, nor did we ever meet most of the students we assisted online. Because of the way SUNY's computing center had configured userids on the VAX—with a combination of initials and social security numbers—we sometimes could not even determine if the email we were reading was composed by a man or a woman.

Email, it seems safe to say, freed both parties from the expressive order of speech, to such a degree that the ritual conventions of identifying oneself or greeting the interlocutor could be forgotten. Email also freed students and tutors from the physical constraints of the writing center. In a sense, you could argue that email tutors and clients had to construct the writing center from their terminals. For some students, email also freed them from the burden of paperwriting, at times, transforming the same terminal that the student wrote monologic papers with into an instrument of dialogic exchange. The following session suggests how that process worked to the student's advantage.

From: In%"444444@albnyvms.Bitnet" 27-sep-1994 20:46:57.17
To: In%"writing@albnyvms.Bitnet"
Subj: How do you choose a subject for a "cultural critique"?

This is for an ENG300Z paper. I really don't know what symbol to grab out of thin air and how to evaluate it in terms of what it "means" or what it reveals about society. HELLLLPPPPPPPP!!!!!!!!!

Bill

From: Albany::writing 27-sep-1994 20:48:49.38
To: In%"444444@albnyvms.Bitnet"
Subj: Re: how do you choose a subject for a "cultural critique"?

Bill,

are you on-line right now? (8:56 pm, tues night) if so , we could talk over vax phone..

—Dave Coogan

From: Albany::writing 27-sep-1994 20:57:36.16
To: In%"444444@albnyvms.Bitnet"
Subj: Re: how do you choose a subject for a "cultural critique"?

Bill,

Why don't you start by telling me more about the assignment. Can this cultural critique be about anything at all? or does it have to address certain issues or reading materials from the class?

When is it due?

(P.S --it's 9:00 pm. I'm logging off now, but I'll check my mail in the morning and respond to whatever you have at that time.)

Good luck, man.

--Dave Coogan

From: In%"444444@albnyvms.Bitnet" 28-sep-1994 14:28:15.85
To: In%"writing@albnyvms.Bitnet"
Subj: Re: how do you choose a subject for a "cultural critique"?

Hi Dave.

sorry - I forgot to mention - first draft is due on Monday. 4-6 pages when it's finished. Final draft due a week from Monday (I think).

The two examples of critical critique we've been given are a British piece about Madonna (even the professor wasn't all that crazy about it) and a more informal piece on how one's wardrobe reflects who one is and how one relates to the current US culture.

As to what we can choose to write about - she has left the field pretty wide open - which for me means I don't know what to write about. The whole idea of digging into the symbols of our culture threatens me. I don't feel like I fit in this culture even though I am a white male from a middle class family. I spent 11.5 years in a Christian drama ministry traveling in Europe and the US - which meant I experienced a lot of culture, but wasn't able to compare it to US culture, only to the culture of the religious group I was traveling with. In the US, the same thing was true.

So. How do I as an "outsider-insider" get a critical handle on what US culture is?

Does that help explain my confusion?

Bill

From: Albany::writing 28-sep-1994 14:46:16.24
To: In%"444444@albnyvms.Bitnet"
Subj: Re: how do you choose a subject for a "cultural critique"?

Bill,

I'm interested in hearing more about why you think that digging into the symbols of our culture is threatening. What do you think you might find? how bad could it be? does a cultural critique have to be negative?

I'm also interested in this Christian drama ministry you describe, and the ways it seems to have "blinded" you from "really seeing" other cultures. I'm skeptical of my own imagery here, as you can probably tell... I wonder why cultural critique always assumes a secular, humanist position.

Maybe you want to critique the idea of cultural critique?

To start, say more about these symbols you're imagining.

--Dave

From: In%"444444@albnyvms.Bitnet" 28-sep-1994 15:36:26.95
To: In%"writing@albnyvms.Bitnet"
Subj: Re: how do you choose a subject for a "cultural critique"?

Well, I'm tempted to shout WHAT SYMBOLS, but -oops, I did. :- (

Digging isn't threatening. Having no concept of what symbols mean to people of this culture is. I'd be trying to pass myself off as a member of a culture I often feel like an alien in. Not an unhappy alien, just an estranged one.

I don't think the professor wants her assignments critiqued. Would you?

Hmmm. What symbols, eh? Well, today the class talked about "grunge" fashion. What does it mean? How should I know? What I wear is whatever I throw on in the morning, or what my wife chooses for me.

See what I mean?

From: Albany::writing 28-sep-1994 18:40:10.31
To: In%"444444@albnyvms.Bitnet"
Subj: Re: how do you choose a subject for a "cultural critique"?

Bill — It sounds like you might begin by writing about why you feel estranged from "this culture." I think a big part of such writing would be defining what culture is.

My guess is that you're talking about the stereotypes of masculinity (since you mentioned being a white male in your last post)... I can understand wanting to resist the way society thinks men should be behave. This would certainly make fine cultural critique if you could focus in on certain symbols or images. A symbol is something that represents something else. So --to use your example--the grunge look is a symbol of.... (and here's where the cultural critique would come in).... a symbol of working class life, of anti-establishment, anti fashion industry, anti-yuppie life.

What images of, say, masculinity or culture can you think of that you might want to write about? In other words, if you do feel estranged from some version of "culture" how would you define this culture, and identify its outward manifestations--its symbols?

--look forward to your response (!)

(I'll be back to check my mail tomorrow morning, first thing.)

--Dave Coogan

From: Albany::writing 30-sep-1994 16:38:34.64
To: In%"444444@albnyvms.Bitnet"
Subj: Re: how do you choose a subject for a "cultural critique"?

Bill,

It was good to meet you today (despite the chaos in the computer room...)
Good luck with your paper.

--Dave

From: In%"444444@albnyvms.Bitnet" 30-sep-1994 20:28:51.74
To: In%"writing@albnyvms.Bitnet"
Subj:

Well, how does one find a symbol to write about?
Dave, you on tonight?

--Bill

From: In%"444444@albnyvms.Bitnet" 1-oct-1994 12:21:13.02
To: in%"writing@albnyvms.Bitnet"
Subj: Hellp!!!!! Dave coogan - are you in on saturdays?

Bill calling Dave. Come in Dave. Over.

I need help with my topic (STILL!) I now have another idea (the europeans view of
the US was unfruitful - I don't really want to write about it.)

I now am thinking about writing about TELEVISION AND SOCIAL
RESPONSIBILITY but most of what I have to say are ideas I developed after reading
Neil Postman's _Entertaining Ourselves To Death_ - a book about how the medium
of television has and is shaping American society. How far can I go in a piece of
expository writing just restating someone else's thoughts expressed in their writing?

Thanks for responding if you get this today. If you get this Monday, don't worry about
it, I had to have the rough draft in by then.

From: Albany::writing 2-oct-1994 13:00:25.34
To: In%"444444@albnyvms.Bitnet"
Subj: Re: hellp!!!!! Dave coogan - are you in on saturdays?

Bill,

Today is Sunday, around 12:45. By now, you may have already narrowed down your
options, but I'll give you my thoughts anyway--for what it's worth now. (if it's any
consolation, I'll be back online tonight if you want to run a draft by me...

It sounds like you've found something you care about in the Postman book. Television seems like a provocative symbol of our society because it simultaneously reflects us and creates us. But this reflection doesn't seem like a direct representation to me: nobody willingly admits that their life has anything to do with the Brady Bunch. But the fact that that show existed says something about our latent identities as Americans (the heterosexual, nuclear family, blonde haired girls, dark haired boys....the whole Ken and Barbie thing.) Perfect people. A symbol of us (?) ...or a symbol of something...

What shows do you watch? What do you know about TV?

Talk to you tonight...

Dave

From: In%"444444@albnyvms.Bitnet" 2-oct-1994 16:26:30.30
To: In%"writing@albnyvms.Bitnet"
Subj: Hi dave coogan. Here's the rough draft. Suggestions on revisions?

WHERE IS THE "CHURCH OF THE OPEN DOOR" ?

Christian churches in the United States today seem very concerned with the number of members that belong to their church, and the number of programs they offer to bring in yet more. A large church, however, does not always equal a church on the same path set forth by the leaders of the early Christian church. In my experience, the percentage of spiritually committed believers is much higher in small or struggling fellowship groups than in large, busy churches.

One of the gauges by which I measure the spiritual health of a Christian fellowship is their willingness to offer hospitality to strangers and to other Christians. In addition to Christ's quoting of the second great commandment "You shall love your neighbor as yourself," there seems to be adequate evidence in the New Testament that hospitality to other Christians as well as to strangers was expected of followers of Jesus Christ in the first century. Both Titus 1:8 and I Tim 3:2 identify hospitality as a necessary quality for anyone seeking to be a Christian leader. Romans 12:13, 1 Peter 4:9 and Hebrews 13:2 each contain an exhortation for all Christians to be hospitable.

For several years I toured here and abroad with a Christian theatre company called the Covenant Players (CP). 4 of those years I was working with CP in the United States: January '79 to December '80, and June '88 to June '90. The group had the opportunity to perform in many Christian organizations—from multi-thousand member churches to small home groups, from working with military chaplains to working with city missions, from working in wealthy Episcopal churches in Boston to performing for small fellowships of coal miners in West Virginia. This afforded us a singular opportunity to obtain a view of what was going on inside the Christian church in the USA.

CP teams had full performances on the average of 2 days a week and spent the rest of the week rehearsing and arranging performances for the next tour. The teams were housed the night before and the night after a performance by families belonging to the church or organization where the performance was held. The income from honorariums and offerings wasn't enough to pay for hostels or motel rooms for the remaining three to five nights a week and all of the other incidental costs of running the tour. For that reason, a team would call a few days ahead to the churches in the area they would be in and ask them to help us by finding a place for our 3 or 4 person team to sleep for 2 or 3 nights.

Each person working with CP knew that our work required acceptance of a simple lifestyle. Most teams I was on were grateful when a church offered to let us use our sleeping bags in a warm carpeted room in their church. Sometimes churches would call families and we were always delighted to learn that they had invited us to stay in their homes. But finding host families with less than a week's notice was not something we expected churches or Christian contacts to do.

Many large churches have comfortable carpeted lounge rooms for the congregation to use for relaxing in between services or for adult Sunday school classes. Others have youth rooms with beaten up, comfortable couches. Some sizable churches have Christian schools with carpeted or uncarpeted classrooms. ALL large churches that I have visited have had SOME carpeted room in them somewhere. If I had chosen to do a statistical survey of the churches which arranged short-notice accommodations for our teams, the overwhelming majority of churches and groups that housed us would be shown to have been smaller or struggling churches, and not the large seemingly successful churches. A few large churches did evidence understanding for outreach of this kind. Much more often, however, leaders of large, flourishing churches we contacted not only wouldn't ask members to house us but told us their church had a rule against allowing anyone to sleep in their church even in a cold uncarpeted room for one night.

On the other hand, we were often amazed at the places where we did find a few night's shelter. Often, a pastor who had a church of less than 50 people would relate strongly to our attempts to live a committed, shoestring lifestyle for God, and would call people in his congregation who would gladly house us—even for the same evening that we were calling if things had gotten that desperate. Once or twice the local homeless mission put us up even though we really weren't homeless and could have paid for a night's housing with monies we had earmarked to get the van repaired or cover some other tour expense.

As I've stated, hospitality seems to have been expected of Christians in the first century church. Through my experiences in Covenant Players, I was cheered to find that hospitality is still a common trait in smaller churches, struggling to know who they are as followers of Jesus Christ. Many large, active churches have special programs designed to invite people to find a "church home" by joining their congregation. Ironically, these same churches often seemed to be the least hospitable to those who were only seeking lodging for one or two nights. It seems that a Christian body that has forgotten who they are called to be for Christ, regardless of their size, have lost the very thing which entitles them to be called Christian.

From: Albany::writing 2-oct-1994 19:18:53.13

To: In%"444444@albnyvms.Bitnet"
Subj: Re: hi dave coogan. Here's the rough draft. Suggestions on revisions?

Bill -- Ok, here's what I got from your draft. (If I can summarize what I understand here).

The symbol that you've identified for cultural critique is the Christian church—specifically, large, mainstream churches. Based on your experience with the theatre group, you claim that small churches are often more hospitable then large churches. Small churches may share more in common with your traveling theatre group ("living on a shoe string for God") and the richer churches...for some reason that I don't think you name... are simply less hospitable.

Your insight seems to be that you can't judge a book by its cover, so to speak: you can't judge a church by its size.

While I appreciate the exposé, I'm not exactly sure how this argument becomes a cultural critique? Perhaps my main difficulty is that I can't see the main-line churches as "symbols" in your argument. I'm not even sure if you're identifying particular churches or not, or simply labeling all big churches as somehow "impostors" or misleadingly spiritual.

I guess I just don't feel the "bite" yet. I understand the topic, but I'm not absolutely sure what the critique is...

--Dave

From: In%"444444@albnyvms.Bitnet" 3-oct-1994 14:13:01.54
To: In%"writing@albnyvms.Bitnet"
Subj: Re: hi dave coogan. Here's the rough draft. Suggestions on revisions?

Success, Dave. The US church rather than contrasting the dominant materialistic US culture buys into the "bigger is better" criterion. Usefulness and meaning don't seem to be major concerns for a SCRATCH LAST 3 WORDS

The church claims to be counter-cultural, yet seems to be a fine example of the all-pervasiveness of American culture. Being closed to strangers or those outside our group, rationalizing a way out of helping those in need around us, and insularity, I see as symptoms of the dominant mainstream white euro-american culture. The church isn't fighting against these things - at least many of the BIG churches aren't. Those churches which are smaller may be more able to be counter culture because they aren't viewed as successful by the greater US Christian community. Does that make sense?

Would you view a 20 person church composed of Senior Citizens in the inner city to be more or less "successful" than Robert Schuller's huge "Crystal Cathedral"?

Bill

From: Albany::writing 3-oct-1994 17:26:19.07
To: In%"444444@albnyvms.Bitnet"
Subj: Re: hi dave coogan. Here's the rough draft. Suggestions on revisions?

Bill,

That's the spirit! Now I'm starting to get a feel for the critique. I sense a fighting spirit, esp. when you label these religions mainstream religions that are insulated,etc. I also liked your question comparing an inner city church with Schuller's Chrystal Cathedral: but now, the burden of your paper will be in defining what successful churches are, and pinning your critique of mainstream, dominant religions to a specific faith. Give me details, details, details. Let's get this critique fired up!

--Dave

This brainstorming session raises a number of interesting points about the methodological differences between talking and writing and their relation to tutor/student roles. A f2f intervention, we might recall, is supposed to teach the student how to change his or her writing process, "to interfere," as North (1984) says, "to get in the way, to participate in ways that will leave the ritual [of composing] itself forever altered" (p. 439). Yet if my comments to Bill changed his composing process, I can honestly say that I don't know what changed. As well, a face-to-face session is supposed to create an expressive order through co-presence. Yet because this session took place over the course of two or three days, entirely in writing, with only one un-related encounter outside of the conference, it is hard to say if or when co-presence occurred, in the traditional sense. Connections are rather fragile: "are you on-line right now?", "are you in on Saturdays?", "I'm logging off now" "Bill calling Dave. Come in Dave. Over."

However, while the pacing is somewhat abrupt, I wouldn't quite say that it represents an aimless movement through the postmodern landscape. In fact, I believe that the loss of an expressive order actually creates a new space for dialogic interaction, driven by what Bakhtin (1981) calls "the ideological becoming of a human being." This process, he says, is one of "selectively assimilating the words of others" (p. 341) in order to produce an internally persuasive discourse that is "tightly interwoven with one's own word" (p. 345). To Bakhtin, discourse is not articulated in a void. It is formed and reformed in relation to the "conceptual horizon" of the other. All discourse, no matter which media it embodies, wagers "an intense struggle within us for hegemony among various available verbal and ideological points of view" (p. 346). The challenge for Bill—which is not activated by email but only exploited by our use of it—is to sort through these competing discourses, including those discourses that Bakhtin says "do not matter to us, that do not touch us" (p. 345).

Some discourses, for example, are inconsequential to Bill. The discourse on clothing and gender does not seem to touch him. "I wear whatever I throw on in the morning, or what my wife chooses for me." Other discourses are not so easily brushed off. There is the discourse of *cultural critique*, which he struggles to populate throughout the exchange; the discourse of *American culture*, which seems to baffle him—the self-proclaimed "outsider–insider;" and the discourse of *Christianity*, as it is articulated by mainstream churches. These discourses present problems to Bill because, in various ways, they appear unmovable, as Bakhtin describes authoritative discourse, as a "compact and indivisible mass," demanding "unconditional allegiance" (p. 343). If Bill is able to flip past the discourse on "grunge fashion," for example, without really seeing it, he lingers, with good reason, on the other discourses, weary of giving over "unconditional allegiance."

The discourse of cultural critique, especially, creates an interesting tension in Bill's posts: "I don't know how to grab a symbol out of thin air." "WHAT SYMBOLS?" he shouts. What am I supposed to do? As he explains later on, "the whole idea" of cultural critique is confusing: "I don't feel like I fit in this culture. To critique it he would have to critique his own privilege as a white, American male—a privilege he does not identify as a privilege, indeed, a "privilege" that seems inscribed upon him, as an authoritative discourse from the class, the teacher, or the readings. Bill cannot be the student he is supposed to be in this assignment—cannot take up the rhetoric of cultural critique—because he cannot assimilate, even if he wants to, a discourse of leftist criticism that baffles and intimidates him. Yet he cannot *not* be a student, as he also makes clear: "I don't think the professor wants her assignments critiqued. Would you?"

Bill's resounding defense of small-scale, Christian ministry becomes, in this way, his own internally persuasive discourse. In choosing this topic, he appears to reconcile the needs of both the centrifugal and the centripetal. By attacking the larger churches, he is able to meet the needs of the assignment—to write a cultural critique—but by choosing a topic that has actually affected his life, as opposed to the topics that were suggested in class, he is able to write from an internally persuasive position. In his last post to me, where he defends himself from my contention that he has not yet written a critique, he starts out with sentences like this:

> Being closed to strangers or those outside our group, rationalizing a way out of helping those in need around us, and insularity, I see as symptoms of the dominant mainstream white euro-american culture.

But then something happens as he writes, and Bill appears to discover a new form of agency:

> Would you view a 20 person church composed of Senior Citizens in the inner city to be more or less 'successful' than Robert Schuller's huge 'Crystal Cathedral'?

This seems to me like one of those moments at a podium where the speaker stops reading from his prepared speech, cocks his head to the side, and finally comes up with the right words. It is interesting to note, in that context, that this sentence was not a part of his formal paper but a part of our email dialogue. It does not belong to the course any more than it belongs to the authorized persona Bill constructs in his paper.

What I say of Bill I might also say of myself. "I wonder" in one of my posts, "why cultural critique always assumes a secular, humanist position." Why can't cultural critique be directed at religion? This question, perhaps, allowed Bill to justify his draft. No doubt I had that in mind when I wrote it. But is this post directed only to Bill? As a graduate student in the same English department, who had encountered the same rhetoric of cultural critique in graduate classes, I shared Bill's resistance to an apparently unmovable, authoritative discourse. Though I might have been more willing than Bill to define "our latent identities as Americans," for example, in relation to such constructs as "the heterosexual, nuclear family," I was, or so it seems to me now, just as much in the process of becoming as the student I was purportedly helping.

DIALOGIC LITERACY IN THE WRITING CENTER

What I value most in email "tutoring," then, is the chance to open up the centrifugal aspects of discourse—to give students and tutors an alternative forum in which to appropriate the discourses that they confront in their education. I am aware, however, that this posture of opening up discourse contradicts our present relations in the apparatus of functional literacy. It disrupts the drive toward centripetal discourse, variously defined as standard written English, academic literacy, disciplinary discourse, and so on. As well, the session with Bill begins to contradict the notion that good writing is a form of independent thinking; that good tutoring is a seamless intervention into that process of thinking. What I will argue, in the remainder of this chapter, however, is that the opposite of independence is not dependence, but what Bakhtin (1990) describes as an ethical obligation to be answerable to the other. This obligation is crucial if we want to create a new apparatus of dialogic literacy in the center. The following session, which I have previously discussed in *Computers and Composition* (Coogan, 1995), suggests one way to do that.

From: ALBANY::555555 21-MAR-1993 19:31:14.38
To: WRITING
Subj: I thought I could I thought I could I thought I could

To: Dave (or whomever else) at WRITING
From: Katie
Re: threat to send sample pages of unmanageable document

Note: I am grad student, ETAP department, preparing a teaching guide, grades 9-12, for a unit on African-American poetry and discrimination. This guide, the main project for an independent study with Africana Studies professor S., utilizes African-American poetry as launching pad for exploring--talking about--discrimination.

Some background: I am hard-wired for chaos. I have learning disabilities and although command of English is not much of a problem, ORGANIZING and maintaining FOCUS are. I am a writer— mostly non-fiction & poetry. TRYING TO ACCOMPLISH TOO MUCH IS A PROBLEM, too.

Specific concerns about sample pages from teaching guide:

1. I think that between preface, introduction, and objectives I have created a monster that is all beginning and no middle.

2. Really want to borrow from what I am learning in CSI 100 (Microcomputing and Disability, Prof. R.) and apply his understanding of disability to discrimination. Also trying to avoid teacher-centered classroom setting, and encourage lots of dialogue, discussion, debate. DO I STATE THESE GOALS OVER AND OVER AND IF SO EVER CLEARLY? My sense is rambling discourse of muttered objectives spread out over too many pages of text.

3. When I get this published, WRITING/ Writing Center will appear among acknowledgements.

4. Keep it simple, how?

5. Can Preface, Intro, Why Black...all merge to one or is it better to keep as is?

THANKS THANKS THANKS!!

PS: "OUTLINE" IS NOT IN MY LEXICON...THE HARD WIRE IS HARD TO CHANGE!

AFRICAN-AMERICAN POETRY AS CATALYST FOR EXPLORING DISCRIMINATION:

A Teaching Guide for a Four-Week Unit on Poetry and Discrimination for Junior and Senior High School Students

AAAS 697 Independent Study and Research
The Poetics of Discrimination

Prof. S.
University at Albany, S.U.N.Y.
Spring 1993

TABLE OF CONTENTS

PREFACE

This teaching guide is the "major project" of an Independent Study and Research course, Poetry and Discrimination, taken during the Spring semester of 1993 at the University at Albany, under the direction of Professor S. of the Africana Studies department. I wanted to continue the reading of African-American poetry begun during AAAS 596, Survey of African-American Literature, focusing on the theme of discrimination. The original title of the course was Poetics and Discrimination, but that changed midstream, because I didn't want to stray too far from the poems themselves, and I had to look at the suitability of Poetics and the reality that the teaching guide, though it could clearly be adaptable for younger or older students, is designed for high school students.

Why this teaching guide? I have a mixture of selfish and altruistic motives. One: I hope to use such a guide in my next career as high school English teacher. In a way, you might say I am making some lesson plans up ahead of time. On a more serious note, my experience has shown me that students--and people in general--either really enjoy poetry, or treat it like some inaccessible alien art form that requires multiple languages for deciphering. (I have always held to the former reaction.) I want poetry to be enjoyable. I also believe strongly in poetry's transformational effects on the heart, mind, and soul. My job, as teacher, is not only to demonstrate that poetry is accessible, but to allow it to work its transformation-empowerment in my students.

Poetics is the art, craft, and mechanics of writing. One goal was to, as much as possible, allow the voices, wisdom, and experience of African-American teacher/writers, such as Langston Hughes and Countee Cullen, shape this guide. I believe an Afrocentric approach to the study of African-American literature is valuable and informative. Work by scholars such as Houston A. Baker, Jr., founder and proponent of African-American poetics and modernism, also focus the look at literature. It would be difficult to utilize African-American poetry as a vehicle for discussion about racial discrimination without the Afrocentric perspective. Such a perspective limits neither the view nor the ability to apply or transfer ideas about discrimination to other forms of discrimination, such as discrimination against the elderly, women, people with functional impairments, the homosexual population, etc. Rather, starting from an Afrocentric point of view, racial discrimination as a theme in African-American poetry is visible in its clearest light; understanding of racial discrimination is most tangible and accessible. The opportunity to transfer insights gained, to look at discrimination through another window, is greater.

INTRODUCTION

This four-week unit utilizes African-American poetry to create discourse in the classroom on the subject of discrimination. University at Albany Professor R.'s understanding of disability as a human-engineered construct, a relationship outside the self, is applied to the working definition of discrimination, asserting that it, too, is a relationship between a person and his goals, needs, opportunities. Just as disability does not reside in the individual who has a functional impairment, discrimination doesn't reside in the person or organization that discriminates, nor in the victim, even though on a personal level the practitioner of discrimination may harbor judgement, prejudice, fear, or ignorance in his heart. The person victimized by the discrimination has feelings as well, but the effect is that the discrimination is a barrier between the victim and her opportunities. Understanding, self-awareness, enlightened attitudes, improved communication skills and changed behavior are all resources to help tear down the barriers.

This guide was not designed with a specific grade level in mind, because prejudice and discrimination are not academic subjects. Prejudice and discrimination are human problems. Its recommended use is for grades nine through twelve; the hope is that the questions, exercises, readings, and assignments are easily adaptable for undergraduate college students, as well.

There is not one right or perfect age at which to begin discussing discrimination. My kindergartener watched the moving PBS special for kids on AIDS featuring Magic Johnson. When she saw the little girl break down, crying and being comforted by Johnson, she felt very sad. I asked her, "Could you play with that little girl...or with any kid who has AIDS?" Her honest five-year-old-not-yet-in-kindergarten answer was, "I don't know. Could I?"

As a loving mother trying to educate my own about something scary, such as AIDS, I reassured her, "Yes, honey. You can play with a kid who has AIDS. You cannot catch it from playing with somebody. You could share a soda, play dolls, play ball, etc." My daughter was greatly relieved. What she doesn't know is that she has met adults and played with kids living with AIDS. There will be a time for full disclosure, but we were trapped by THE SECRET being guarded by the children's parents and our desire that they first experience these kids as kids first, not kids defined or qualified by something.

We all need to be ourselves first. Therein lies the magic blueprint for creating a place within where justice can dwell, from which we can clean house, ridding our hearts of the fears, misconceptions, and misunderstandings that separate us from our brothers and sisters. The Christian Church (as well as other faiths) offers that opportunity, but

Christ's teachings are not appropriate in public schools. There has to be a secular way for educators to exorcise the disease of prejudice and liberate truth from the souls we teach. One such way, is to teach the history of the Civil Rights Movement. Because African-American poetry is the vehicle for this exploration of discrimination, we will most closely examine racial discrimination; however, there will be opportunities to open the discussions and exercises to discrimination against the homosexual population, people with functional impairments, and those with varying ethnic and religious backgrounds. Teachers need to make the material as applicable to their students' lives as possible, for the express purpose of ownership; we may confront students who deny having a relationship to racial discrimination, who claim they have never experienced it, witnessed it, etc. The lesson plans that follow are designed to help students recognize that they already have a relationship to discrimination--that all have felt first hand its sting, or witnessed its sting, or inflicted its sting.

Public school teachers, whether working in Alaska, the South Bronx, or Yeehaw Junction, Florida need to incorporate dialogue on prejudice and discrimination throughout grade levels and throughout the school year; such topics should not just be hauled out, dusted off, and paid attention to during February, Black History Month. IF WE DO NOT STUDY HISTORY, WE ARE DOOMED TO REPEAT IT. (Find source of this quote...) Martin Luther King, Jr. drove home to this nation and the world that "injustice anywhere...(look up & correct quote, prob. from Stride Toward).......". " We should not be engaging students in dialogue on discrimination because it is politically correct, we should be challenging students to confront their own prejudices and painful experiences with discrimination because HUMAN SURVIVAL, BROTHER AND SISTERHOOD, DEPEND ON IT. As Martin Luther King stated, "We can choose to walk the high road of human brotherhood or to tread the low road of man's inhumanity to man." ("Where Do We Go from Here?" (Stride Toward Freedom)

If that is accepted, there really is no proper age at which to begin the education. Because I am a poet, student of African-American poetry, and future teacher of English to grades 6-12, I have personal, academic, and professional reasons for preparing this teaching guide.

The focus of this guide is less to teach poetry as genre, and more to explore discrimination, in particular racial discrimination. Yet there is a language to studying poetry, and the success of the recommended poems as launch pads depends on some common poetry language. The suggested readings can and should be studied for their own contributions to literature written in the English language, but herein serve as catalysts, or vehicles for creating opportunities in which students can explore discrimination: their experiences with it, their relationship to it, and their feelings about it. While prejudice arises out of ignorance and fear, and is inexorably linked to such inward things as feelings and beliefs; discrimination involves words, events, actions, practices, and deeds. Discrimination is the outward manifestation of prejudice. It is an outside, human-engineered construct, a relationship between an individual and his or her needs, opportunities, and goals.

WHY BLACK POETRY

African-American poetry offers a wealth of backdrops, of points of departure; the case can be made that it is a more truly American poetry, say, than many of the

American poets taught, for many American poets were heavily influenced by the British masters. African-American poetry is wed to the history of racial oppression and apartheid in America. Thus, African-American poetry is specifically selected as the vehicle for this inquiry because:

1. Most works are relatively short, manageable units accessible to readers of various abilities. Unlike a novel in which a learning disabled student, for example, might get lost, a poem could be read aloud in the beginning of the class, giving all a common reference and point of departure.

2. Poetry allows students to begin exploring the sensitive issue of discrimination from a safe place outside him or herself. While it is hoped that students would take risks sharing their experience, strength, and hope with each other, a poem provides a safe beginning place.

3. The wealth of appropriate selections from works by African-American poets constitute a wealth of truly American literature that is underread by high school students.

4. The history of racial discrimination in America is a dominent theme in African-American literature.

5. Studying African-American poetry offers students a chance to take a few steps in someone else's shoes. The Civil Rights Movement is not a movement designed to benefit one group of people; yet, because of the suffrage of Black Americans, many others have directly benefitted. America's disabled citizens could not have fought for civil rights, accessible work and learning environments had the road not been paved by their African-American brothers and sisters.

From: WRITING 23-MAR-1993 19:31:14.38
To: 555555
Subj: I thought I could I thought I could I thought I could

Katie-- Wow, quite a project. Allow me to cut to the chase, though, and let you know what happened to me when I read this section of your paper.

I was immediately impressed with the scope of your paper—discrimination AND poetry—and I was taken by your tact and sensitivity. You don't seem to be out on a PC kick or any other indoctrination trip. That much is clear. You also seem clear about poetry—that is, you've narrowed down poetry to a specific sort of writing—a definition of poetry—this project. If I were a teacher reading the proposal, I'd assume I might get specific ways to teach specific poems to elicit not so specific "reactions" to discrimination. I also get the idea that I could apply those poems—extend their analogy—to other forms of discrimination besides race. On the whole, then, your thinking is pretty straight forward and your motives are not muddy at all.

Your writing, however, could be a bit tighter—shorter, less ambitious, with more quotes and illustrations, more narrative (like the story about your daughter) and less theoretical explanation. You are, as far as I can make out, trying to "sell" this unit to teachers. Probably the best way to do that is to stick to a clear -albeit simple- story and put the theory in its place; subordinate the theory to your motives, structurally...that is, physically, in the text.

As you anticipated, the main work to be done is organization. I often have the same problem in my own writing. As you've probably already discovered, it's helpful to hear how someone else might orginanize. (I do this all the time). So here's how I'd do it for your proposal:

Instead of intro, preface, etc. and all those numbers, I'd do 2 sections.

1.   Why study discrimination? 2 paragraphs max

This section would be a rationale —a defense of the topic against PC, and your interpretation of the afro centric tradition. I was a little confused with your "explantion" of this. I need to know more how YOU interpret this tradition. if it is a monolithic, stable tradition, i'd like to know the basic beliefs, hear some quotes, or get something meaty. perhaps, also, an historical context (like your quotes from King, Marshal, etc)

2.   My angle in this project: how will I address discrimination?

If the first section is more theoretical —clearing the table— this section would be more of a story. It should be longer and bounce along, as it does with that story about you and your child. Teachers will probably respond to this better than the rationale because they

a.   ALREADY want to address discrimination and will skip over the rationale to get to your story and the how-to

b.   or they are apathetic to your proposal from the start, and no rationale —no matter how tactful, forceful, thorough, or tough— will sell them. The only hope for this group is to sucker 'em with a story

Given this situation with the audience, I think you need to get to the poetry and the how-to-teach poetry and discrimination awareness as soon as possible.

In fact, if you can find a way to incorporate the theory into the narrative and simply condense the whole thing by half, you could probably get away with omitting a rationale section. It would probably be smoother. And then you could address some more issues such as your relation to the afro american perspective. You might address the deceiving simplicity of poetry's "transformational effects on the heart, mind and soul." I'm not doubting that they exist, necessarily, but I think the project hinges upon this and from the introduction, I don't sense you have examined your own facile identification of "wisdom" in poetry and their effects on heart, mind and soul. If poetry is such an animal, and you either love it (because you can undertand how it talks to your heart) or you hate it (you just don't get it) then how can you claim later that poetry offers students a "safe" place for them to step outside themselves? How can poetry be simultaneously safe AND powerful? Should teachers think of poetry as a harmless little text that they can mold and manipulate or a powerful, daunting voice that yanks our hearts all by itself?

Let me know how it goes --address further correspondence or further drafts to me, unless of course, if you want another perspective. Either way.

Good luck--Dave

From: ALBANY::555555 22-MAR-1993 22:59:58.50
To: WRITING
Subj: Gratitude

Hi Dave, thanks for your thoughtful & thorough response. You asked really good questions (or made helpful comments) especially re: can poetry be safe and powerful. Lots to think about...Be prepared for further drafts & lesson plans. Am very very grateful I took the risk—it was scary to ask for help & am glad I did.--Katie

---

From: ALBANY::555555 23-MAR-1993 08:33:15.76
To: WRITING
Subj: PS

Hi Dave...had another thought re: the help. One of my LD/ADD related impairments is that I process info. slowly. The on-line help provides written record of the help to which I can refer, read, read again, digest. I can better utilize understand & apply the comments because of the record. I also have some troublew/ auditory processing, e.g. if the writing center were busy (note: I am not really familiar w/ the layout of W.C.) the other sounds 1. could distract me
from the comments, and 2. for me, one incoming sound or noise can compete w/ another and the effect is neither is understood...On-line isn't just great for us chickens, it's great for learning disabled students, too.

From: ALBANY::555555 29-MAR-1993 08:52:35.33
To: WRITING
Subj: Take 2...? in progress

March 29, 1993

To: Dave at WRITING
From: Katie
RE: Rewrite in progress 3/27-29/93

Hi Dave--back to all the good help you offered: you sure asked a good question! Like any incompetent teacher, I am going to pass it on to the students by including it in my teaching guide:
Can poetry be both safe and powerful?

The answer is yes, but it does depend on how we define "safe."

I am not thinking about the no-risk taking, automoton in nirvana kind of safety. Ever read Madeleine L'Engle's A Wrinkle in Time? How safe were the inhabitants of Camazotz (spelling) ??? What kinds of feelings did they experience? I think that kind of "safety" is really stasis, shelter--at best. For the Camazotz dwellers under rigid control and strict oppression by the evil IT, that "safety" is much worse.

What I mean by safety is a safe environment in which to share, grow, take risks. A classroom in which there are accepted ground rules, such as no judging one another. A classroom in which there are no stupid questions. A classroom in which the teacher doesn't know everything. A classroom with a teacher who serves more as facilitator, respondent. (Respondent, that's a good one. It's academic conferese for he or she who facilitates the paper- presenters.)

The thought was that to start the unit launching into, "OK, Class, what's YOUR relationship to discrimination?" would be an assault, followed by the arms flatly folded across the chest, and no takers.

African-American poetry is profoundly influenced by the history of oppression; racial discrimination remains a dominent theme in the literture. I thought that there would be some comfort level, some initial distance in looking at Black poetry. Need I rethink this? Although the readings may have a powerful effect, it couldn't be precisely the individual student's story--even if there is strong identification.

I guess the kind of safety I envision is the kind of safety one finds in the following possible locations:

a.   a school or place of worship, listening to a talk, sermon, lecture or reading that challenges old ideas
b.   group psychotherapy (SOMEHOW thereapists create a safe place inwhich people can work through powerful issues in their lives...)
c.   support groups, or 12-Step programs, in which people find courage to share and hear things that aren't always comfortable or "nice"

--And YES, I am aware that teacher does not equal therapist. Yet teachers need to be concerned with creating that environment for students that is conducive to asking questions, sharing

themselves and their stories, etc.
--Katie

From: WRITING 31-MAR-1993
To: 555555
Subj: RE: REWRITE IN PROGRESS

Katie: I guess I need to know more about the destiny of this document --or the intended destiny. Is it for you? Notes for your own classroom agenda? If so, then I think it's sound. Is that intended to convince teachers --rhetorically convince teachers-- to take up a unit on Black poetry? Or is it your way of working out your pedagogy?

What I'm getting at is this: if you want to convince other people to take up this unit I think you need to be more brief, more explicit, and less dramatic. For example, the paragraphs that began with "the single most important thing we can do for humanity" began to feel like a cliche. I'm sure that within the context of teaching, students might agree with your solution --to listen more, share, etc. But as an academic argument, I think you need more.

Anyway, I'd be happy to talk more. WRITING will be down Thurs-Sun but back (sporadically) on Spring Break. Take care --Dave

---

From: ALBANY::555555 21-APR-1993
To: WRITING
Subj: Belated Thanks to Dave

Hi Dave, sorry not to have thanked you sooner for the help re: draft 2. I have a variety of reasons for not responding sooner, the most honest is I felt really discouraged--you pointed out a real problem--is it a bunch of lesson plans or a pedagogy. I am not sure. End of semester is 2 weeks away...Revamped the paper starting as you suggested. May forward it to you for another look. Are you inundated with submissions to WRITING? I have referred a log of lot of folks. Thanks, Katie

---

From: ALBANY::555555 21-APR-1993 22:46:06.83
To: WRITING
Subj: PS

hi dave, the good news is the prof. saw draft 3 and really likes the project, so it doesn't matter if i resovle the pedagogy vs. lesson plan issues right now. Ditched prose poem--one of those asides from academic reality. You helped more than I can

express. Thanks. Is Writing avail. during summer sessions, I hope? Tell your
supervisor the demand is great. Take care!

In some ways, this session does not appear to be much different from the previous session. Like Bill, Katie uses her draft and her email about her draft to cut some
kind of path through the heteroglossia of discourses that surround her. Like Bill, she
makes no attempt to hide the ways in which she is variously situated, in this case, as
a graduate student, a teacher-to-be, a poet, a scholar, a crusader against discrimination, and a person with learning disabilities. My responses to Katie also indicate
that I am invested in what she is saying, from my own positioning as a scholar, a
poet, a graduate student, and a teacher-to-be. Our positions may differ, but because
of our similar backgrounds as students, they are necessarily in flux: We both use
email to work out our own internally persuasive discourses about these topics we
care about.

The way in which this session works, however, is different from the way in
which the previous session works, because here we use email to directly sustain an
ethical obligation to each other. At first glance, of course, the session may appear
unethical, at least by traditional standards. Tutors are not supposed to become invested in the content of the student's paper. But the real struggle, here—the heart of
dialogic literacy—is not to make Katie more confident of her own opinions, but to
make both of us answerable to each other's opinions. The relationship is not so
much tutor to student as it is writer to writer, teacher to teacher, poet to poet. What's
required here is not an ethic of intervention but a rhetoric of answerability.

In Bakhtin's (1990) work, answerability arises out of the "ever-present excess of
my seeing, knowing, and possessing in relation to any other human being" (p. 23).
This excess is not a rare commodity. It is "founded in the uniqueness and irreplace-
ability of my place in the world" (p.23). Since none of us occupy the same place in
the world, the excess of seeing is rather common. "When I contemplate a human being," he writes,

> I shall always see and know something that he, for his place outside and over against
> me, cannot see himself: parts of his body that are inaccessible to his own gaze (his
> head, his face, and its expression), the world behind his back, and a whole series of
> objects and relations, which at any of our mutual relations are accessible to me but not
> to him" (p. 23).

Although Katie and I do not literally see the world behind each other's backs, we
nevertheless see, or choose to see, "a whole series" of "relations" in our posts that
the other one cannot see. We both have an excess of seeing in relation to the other
but not the same excess; we don't see the same things. The session works because of
these differences, not in spite of them. For example, when Katie insists that "we
should be challenging students to confront their own prejudices and painful experi-

ences with discrimination" I raise the specter of political correctness. Where she assumes a friendly audience of teachers who would be persuaded by a rhetoric of "we should," I assume a skeptical bunch that needs to be "suckered with a story." Similarly, when she claims that poetry can have "transformational effects on the heart, mind, and soul" and then later claims that poetry can provide students with a "safe place outside him or herself" I take the opportunity to ask her how poetry can be both safe and powerful.

The point of these comments is not to engage a dialectical pursuit of the truth. The point is to dialogize our interaction, in part, by scrutinizing the boundaries of what we see, by seeing it in relation to another. The reason Katie finds some of my posts useful, then, is not because she agrees with me but because she sees herself refracted through me. As Bakhtin (1990) has argued, our excess of our seeing is useful for ideological becoming only if we "return into ourselves" and "consummate the material we derived from projecting ourselves into the other" (p. 26). Likewise, without Katie, my questions about poetry or teaching would not have been written, and I would have lost an opportunity for dialogic growth. As it turns out, her paper provoked me to respond outside the role of the generalist tutor—to write about the teaching of African-American poetry as if it were my paper, too; to write, as well, from that part of my "self" that studies poetry and poetics, both as a literature student and a writer. There is a difference, says Nancy Welch (1993) in an essay on responding to student writing, between "a genuine question" and a question "masquerading beneath a question mark"—between an effort "to create meaning from a text's many voices" and an effort to conceal "the dynamic interplay among many voices" (pp. 498–499). In this case, the difference is in the way I construct myself not just as a "tutor" but as a reader.

In turn, Katie was challenged to do more than just make corrections or organizational changes, but to re-phrase or re-articulate her beliefs. Although she did make those structural changes, as readers can see from consulting the Appendix, she did not stop there. What I want to emphasize is that when she took the opportunity to question her ideas, she did not do so in the formal paper but in email: "what I mean by safety is a safe environment" for students to take risks. "I thought that there would be some comfort level, some initial distance in looking at Black poetry. Need I rethink this?" This last comment is intriguing, in part, because it indicates some discomfort with her appropriation of Black poetry. Katie also seems to be saying that she wants to reconsider the larger issues, but not if it means jeopardizing the argument in her paper. What, then, is the relation between the Katie who writes the paper and the Katie who writes the email; between the self who sees Black poetry as an all purpose vehicle for discussing discrimination in the public schools, and the self who is not so sure anymore that her use of Black poetry or her construction of the "safe" classroom will work?

In my email, I probe the issue by asking Katie about the "intended destiny" of the paper. "Is it for you? Notes on your own classroom agenda?" Or is it "intended to convince teachers—rhetorically convince teachers—to take up a unit on Black Poetry?" After several weeks on inactivity in the session, Katie told me that this comment "really discouraged" her: "You pointed out a real problem." The problem, however, is not so much with the academic argument, but with her personal relation to the argument. If my comment got under her skin, it seems reasonable to ask which skin, which self, which writer was affected. Likewise, if I cared enough to write and rewrite those responses to Katie about the relationship between poetics and politics, it seems reasonable to assume that Katie's merging of the two—in a sense, her willingness to collapse poetics into politics—got under my skin, also in a generative way.

WHO GETS TO BE DIALOGIC IN THE CENTER?

In dialogic literacy, it follows then, that the email "tutor" does not approach "the writer" from the sidelines, determined to sustain the student's academic persona. The goal is not to preserve the fiction of the argument or "the one" making the argument but to complicate both in such a way that the student and the tutor will have opportunities to think differently about themselves-in-writing. Email "tutoring" becomes a collaborative activity where both parties become answerable to the other, connecting through those unauthorized, unofficial selves haunting the margins of the formal paper. Which raises a very practical question: Is this a writing center activity?

Of course, I would not be writing this book if I did not believe writing centers should engage the dialogic: I would not make the effort if I had no interest in seeing peer tutors become technoprocateurs. I understand, however, that in order to see this particular version of the future, I need to see beyond what currently exists in the writing center, in writing programs, in computers and composition, and in higher education. There are several issues to be addressed, in other words, if email tutoring is to be implemented in anything but experimental ways. Because I will address the larger framework of Composition Studies toward the end of the book, I would like to focus my attention, here, on the relationship between dialogic literacy and electronic mail.

First, there is the issue of conference methodology. For some, the relative anonymity of email may appear to reverse North's famous bumper sticker motto for writing centers ("Our job is to produce better writers, not necessarily better writing"), giving too much importance to the writing, at the expense of "the writer." Email, I would agree, makes it difficult to essentialize "the writer" or the writer's world. When the writer *becomes* his or her writing online, however partially or tenuously—and that writing keeps changing from draft to draft and message to message—the idea of "the writer" also seems to change. Each message, rather than confirming The Self, (potentially, at least) produces different versions of the self, which tutors must make sense of, or somehow read *as texts*. Similarly, email calls into question the so-called pure, unmediated space of traditional conferences, drawing attention to the performative nature of all types of face-work. In my view, however, this is a positive development for a *writing* center, because it funnels the social energy of talk into the activity of writing.

Second, some may argue that the Bakhtinian aspects of email "tutoring" represent nothing more than the latest privilege of literacy. This is especially damaging in terms of instruction, because unlike conversation, email places new financial, procedural, and pedagogical hurdles before that student and the tutor. With the exception of remote users who can't come to the campus writing center, then, email adds an extra layer to the tutorial process that does not need to be there. Perhaps it is okay to value dialogic literacy in a population of advanced writers like Bill and Katie who have proper access to computers. But it is questionable to offer it to poorly prepared writers who have little or no access to computers. Since traditional writing centers have been set up to help poorly prepared writers, it would seem as if email does not serve egalitarian ends, at least not in the tutorial process: If the medium has a message, then that message is exclusion.

This criticism is more compelling than the first because it appeals not only to common sense but to the writing center's history and solidarity with poorly prepared writers. Of course, I don't want to underestimate the economic and political difficulties of securing proper computer access for students. But I feel it is misleading to reduce the question of access to a state of possession. When someone does not have access to computer technology, in this case, email, they lack much more than a machine but a range of literacy practices. Students have practical access to email, but they may not have ideological access to dialogic literacy, as I suggest in the next chapter. To address the question of access, then, we need to address much more than the practical questions regarding campus networking, user training, platform compatibility, and so on, but the ideological questions that are at the heart of any discussion of technology: In this case, what *are* the legitimate uses of email in college writing instruction? Who gets to be dialogic in the center? If it seems impossible to imagine dialogic literacy amongst a population of less-able, poorly prepared writers, what does this say about the way the writing center has been constructed and the way we legitimatize that construction?

A third objection to email "tutoring" and dialogic literacy is that, however interesting it may be, it is simply not practical or worth the effort. We are too busy and too under-staffed to allow peer tutors, graduate T.A.s, or even adjunct instructors to write a lot of email back and forth with students. Though it may be enriching to open up the borders between ourselves and others, as Bakhtin suggests, this fluid movement is not possible in the hustle and bustle of most writing centers.

Though it seems like a shallow criticism—really, a shrug of the shoulders—I believe this is the most serious criticism because it condones the ways students tend to see writing as an emergency—something that needs to be handled quickly. Even when students manage to come to the writing center before that critical period, they come to end writing, not to expand it. They are often, but not always, disappointed when they realize they will have to write another draft. The problem with setting up new situations for dialogism, then, has to do with this inevitable closure that is forced upon writing in the university. For example, in the case of Katie, as soon as the professor saw the paper and authorized it, the session ended. Ordinarily, this would not be a problem. But in the context of dialogic literacy, closure can be problematic: "it doesn't matter," according to Katie, "if i resolve the pedagogy vs. lesson plan issues right now." The point is that I'm done.

Perhaps, you might think, I'd be happy with this ending—pleased to see Katie reach her goals. But my experience tells me that while we kept that particular session going—while we wrote that email and re-read each other's questions—we kept ourselves open to the possibility that the utterance could be understood differently; that our conceptions of pedagogy, poetics, and discrimination could be reconceived or refracted through each other. If I can put it in axiomatic form: Closure deferred breeds respect for difference. When we trust each other to respect the incommensurable, we can tolerate a great deal of dissensus online. And that can be most generative.

Yet the rituals of paperwriting in higher education appear to work against this kind of generative dissensus. In a paper, you need to come to the point, as soon as possible. Contradictions or reversals are interpreted as signs of weakness. Collaboration, likewise, is another sign of weakness: Collaborative writing centers, according to many professors, are for those writers who can't contain contradictions, control their arguments, or in other ways prove themselves, independently. They are for writers who find it hard to be writers. Of course, a writing center, on its own, cannot change the way paperwriting works in the academy, but as I hope I've proven in this chapter, it can interrupt the race toward closure through dialogic, email encounters.

To do this, however, writing centers need to confront what appears to be sacred ground: the face-to-face writing conference. When we in writing centers claim the face-to-face conference—flag pushed deep into the soil of Composition Studies—we are essentially claiming the right to do things "for" students. The tendency, I know, is to pretend, that writing centers are student-centered in the strictest sense; that students really want their writing centers—indeed, that writing centers could exist naturally or even spontaneously, without directors or budgets or university-wide articulations of literacy. That we manage to collect the social energy of peer networks into the idea of the writing center is impressive. But at the same time, I would like to argue, politely, that the Neil Armstrong-moment of unfurling the traditional writing center flag—admittedly, one small step forward for students—is not necessarily a giant step forward for college writing.

What I want to stick up for, then, is a new type of stewardship for writing that transcends but does not ignore the limits of paperwriting. That I see this stewardship carried out in electronic forums may seem like a radical departure and, in some ways, it is. But ultimately, it is not a departure from print or a departure from f2f conferencing. It is a departure from the Strategy of Containment. In that light, it should be understandable that when some students and tutors fail to engage a rhetoric of answerability online, that failure says much more about the ISA of literacy than it does about computers. At stake is not just procedural access to email but ideological access to dialogic literacy.

In the next chapter, I will address the question of failure in more depth, analyzing those sessions in which the students were not as well positioned as Bill or Katie to practice dialogic literacy. There, I hope to establish the limits of email as a "revolutionary" technology by foregrounding those non-technological aspects of change that are, in my opinion, much more entrenched and, hence, much more difficult to refigure.

3

The Medium is Not the Message

Tools of inscription embody and construct ideological practices, redefining what exists, what is good, and what is possible to do. But understanding the opportunities and transformations that the tools themselves may offer cannot fully explain or predict their effects on the world. Technologies, after all, arise out of and operate within already existing social, political, and economic relations, practices already imbued with ideology. In the tension between the new potentialities they offer and the ideological formations within which they have been created, new tools . . . often foreground ideological conflicts.

— (Kaplan, 1991, p. 21)

As Nancy Kaplan suggests, writing technologies often foreground particular visions of the good, the possible, and the meaningful. But as she also makes clear, such visions are usually accompanied by a fissure between technological possibility and ideological reality. Thus, while email can, in some cases, enable tutors and students to think together in non-foundational ways; to pursue dissensus generatively, with a common understanding that disagreements can spur growth, email cannot produce such results. No one, as Kaplan says, can really predict how writing technologies and people will interact. But in the long run, I believe we will be able to form more reasonable expectations of email "tutoring" and dialogic literacy if we can distinguish both from the Rhetoric of Technocentrism. Or, to put it another way, we might gain more insights into the medium of email if we resist concluding that the medium is the message.

In an interview, Marshall McLuhan once explained his famous aphorism this way: "I have insisted that any new structure for codifying experience and moving information, be it alphabet or photography, has the power of imposing its structural character and assumptions upon all levels of our private and social lives—even without benefit of concepts or of conscious acceptance" (Bendetti and DeHart, 1996, p. 106). What interests me, here, is the McCarthy-like suspicion of the media; the notion that it can infiltrate our way of life, inconspicuously, without our knowledge or participation. Christina Haas (1996) has dubbed this the myth of all-powerful technology, which is related, perhaps paradoxically, to another myth of transparent technology. Both "compel us to remain noncritical" (p. 35) of our own relations with technologies, albeit in different ways. "More specifically," Haas argues, both myths "take people out of the realm of technology development, technological critique, and technological inquiry and set them in positions to be merely receivers or consumers of technology" (p. 33). Like the apparatus of functional literacy, which takes a purely instrumental approach to language, these myths remove the social or ideological contexts of technology from view, leaving us with two options: Technology changes everything or technology changes nothing; either it is all powerful and autonomous, or it is inconsequential and invisible. Obviously, these are lousy options.

In order to pursue dialogic literacy in the electronic writing center, at the very least, we need a critical theory of technology. Stuart Blythe (1997), following Andrew Feenberg, describes one version of that theory as "a conceptual space" where writing centers can "envision and shape new forms of technology that meet desired educational goals" (p. 103). Instead of assuming, in other words, that technology changes nothing or that it changes everything, writing centers should assume more of an active role in shaping technology, in its design and application, so that "it follows more democratic, empowering paths" (p. 104). Although there will always be room to debate what is meant by such terms as empowerment or democracy, the larger point is that there is, indeed, a nexus of human agency, political realities, and technological possibilities. Against the Rhetoric of Technocentrism, or any all-or-nothing approach, we need to theorize this nexus so that we might better understand how agency is constructed and how change comes about in online environments.

Perhaps the easiest way to support that premise is to illustrate the dangers of avoiding it. It was not that long ago, for example, that Thomas Farrell (1978) critiqued the liberal, NCTE document Students' Right to Their Own Language by referring to "the" technology of literacy. Building on Walter Ong's (1982) claim that "writing restructures consciousness," Farrell made it clear that spoken dialects, including those of minority speakers, were simply not comparable to "the" writing system; that however much we may appreciate differences in spoken dialect, "there are optimum conditions that speed up the visual processing of the written language, and the regularized conventions of Edited American English (EAE) are part of those optimum conditions" (p. 347). The emphasis here on "optimum conditions" for "processing" suggests that literacy is an autonomous technology. "All other things being equal," Farrell concluded, "regularized forms of writing are less distracting and more predictable than irregular forms—and therefore easier for readers to process cognitively" (p. 347).

Of course, as Beth Daniell (1986), J. Elspeth Stuckey (1991), Richard Ohmann (1985), and others have argued, all things are *not* equal. What amazes Daniell, for example, is the thoroughness with which Ong and Farrell will find in the history of writing a "neutrality where none exists" (p. 188). Many literacy theorists, including Ong and Farrell,

> seem so committed to the notion of literacy as causal, rather than enabling . . . that they minimize the social forces which encourage or restrict not only literacy but also cognitive styles. Proponents of the Great Leap see, instead, social conditions as consequences of literacy. They fail to see what other scholars, like Resnick and Resnick, Eisenstein, Oxenham, Stubbs, Street, and Heath . . . have pointed out so clearly: that is precisely social conditions that determine what counts as literacy, who has access to literacy, and what uses and functions literacy can be put to. (p. 188)

By re-inserting human agency into the equation, Daniell politicizes the technology of literacy. In so doing, she reminds us what is really at stake in any reconfiguration of literacy online. When we ignore the social or ideological history of technology, we become susceptible to the idea that the technology of literacy, as Ohmann says, "somehow came before *someone's* intentions to enable *some* minds to do *some* things" (p. 681). What would have happened, he speculates, if writing "had been invented by slaves—say, in the Roman Empire—and for purposes of survival, resistance, and rebellion? . . . . (or suppose) "that wireless communication had evolved, not under the guidance and for the needs of the British Navy, the United Fruit Company, and commercial advertisers, but among women tinkering in their homes, sharing knowledge about domestic production, establishing networks of childcare and concern" (p. 680). That we find these scenarios difficult to imagine should not be surprising. The difficulty, I suspect, does not come when we fathom *why* but when we fathom *how*: these groups could have appropriated the new technologies of representation, given the social constraints in their lives. Of course, the problem here, as it is in any discussion of the effects of the ISA of literacy, is that *why* and *how* are intertwined, as the superstructure and the infrastructure are intimate partners in the interpellation of the subject.

As I argued in Chapter One, this subject has not been created by English departments alone but by a much broader range of stakeholders inside and outside the university. Searching for the origins of this apparatus, however, is a lot like searching for those roots in the family tree that no one wants to talk about. Unwavering genealogists such as David Russell and Cheryl Geisler, however, have identified these roots with the development of the modern university, itself: the professionalization of the faculty, the increasing power of accrediting agencies, changes in size and composition of the student-body, and the growing link between education and upward mobility. In this environment, according to Geisler (1994), the problem of literacy soon became characterized by a "Great Divide" between university experts and lay persons.

Because the academic disciplines, as Russell (1991) makes eminently clear throughout his curricular history on WAC, have been locked in this epic struggle between the forces of access and the forces of exclusion, rhetorical instruction that would demystify academics and widen the net of inclusion, remains a controversial prospect. It is no wonder, then, that literacy is still located, almost exclusively, in the freshman year, at the cusp of students' conflicting identifications with their indigenous cultures and the professional cultures of the university; no wonder that curricular efforts to link literacy with the academic disciplines have been fraught with difficulty; no wonder that even when universities do develop writing-across-the-curriculum programs, they often sustain their freshman writing programs, apparently, finding the contradiction between these two models of literacy easier to deal with than the political fallout of dropping "basic" writing from the requirements.

To penetrate the disciplines with literacy, in other words, one would not only need to penetrate the ISA of functional literacy but the Great Divide, as well. One would have to address the problem of students' access to the disciplines via the rhetoric of the disciplines. Throughout most students' educational lives, however, as Geisler points out, knowledge rarely has a rhetorical dimension, either in textbooks, examinations, or writing assignments. Students are not taught how to create new facts but to revere those facts that experts have created. This situation "practically guarantees that experts will be the only ones who are able to use a field's texts in any kind of sophisticated manner" (p. 94). Ultimately, what a student learns from this situation is not a set of facts but a way of respecting the expert who creates the facts.

I am not interested in making a categorical argument against expertise or disciplinarity. Nor do I see the issue plainly, as a matter of increasing access to the disciplines. Yet I will agree with Geisler's conclusion that, when it comes to undergraduate education, "such exclusionary practices cry out for reform" (p. 94), particularly if we have other goals in mind for our students in addition to inculcating a respect for expertise. In this chapter, then, I will explore the limits of the expert/layperson divide, as it recreates itself in the so-called revolutionary space of the email "tutorial." I begin, in other words, where we happen to find ourselves, at the borders of the academic disciplines, where students and tutors strive to understand what experts understand only tacitly: the rhetorical aspects of making knowledge, or more cynically, the rules of academic gamesmanship.

From: "AW9999@ALBNYVMS.BITNET" 21-FEB-1995 11:26:17.69
To: "writing@ALBNYVMS.Bitnet"
Subj: essay

I have trouble writing a coherent essay. My ideas jump from one thing to another. I have had papers dropped a letter grade because of the problem. I have an essay exam on 2/23. How would you approach a question like this? Popular democrates are ensnared in a dilemma of federalism. What is the dilemma, how is the dilemma related to changes in the political since the founding? Do you think there is a way out why or why not?

I also have the same problem with an english essay due 2/28. The question: discuss the portrait of the family in the 20th century american drama, what are the primary similarities and differences between the portrayals you have chosen and what might these be attributed? What do you think? I would appreciate a reply as soon as possible.

From: ALBANY::WRITING 21-FEB-1995 15:24:20.20
To: "AW9999@ALBNYVMS.Bitnet"
Subj: RE: essay

Dear AW,

Yes, indeed. Coherence is hard to achieve in writing. It's also a fickle thing.... what one professor thinks is coherent, another may think is inchoherent. Part of the problem is the way people interpret a text. But there are, nevertheless, things we can work on to find coherence. I find, however, that I need to spend a lot of time being incoherent when I'm just starting an assignment and then later, when I revise, I work towards coherence.

Whey don't we start with the essay test question.

This question begins with an assertion, "Popular democrats are ensnared in a dilemma of federalism." Do you agree with the assertion? And how would you define "popular democrats" and "federalism"? I would begin answering the question by trying to define these terms and trying to establish if the assertion is true or false. Then I would move to the follow up questions, "What is the dilemma, how is the dilemma related to changes in...." and so on.
Perhaps we could work on this right here in e-mail. How would you define these terms?

****

And now, the paper question:

The way I read this question, we first need to agree that there is a single portrait of the american family in the 20th century. If we agree that such a portrait exists, then we need to construct it. Try sketching a portrait, making reference to one of the works you've read, and I'll do my best to help you develop it into a coherent essay. Deal?
--Dave Coogan

From: ALBANY::WRITING 22-FEB-1995 12:10:47.40
To: "AW9999@ALBNYVMS.Bitnet"
Subj: RE: essay

A.W., Did you get my mail about your essay assignments? And, would you like to discuss the projects? or do you feel comfortable with your approach at this time? --Dave

From: "AW9999@ALBNYVMS.BITNET" 22-FEB-1995 13:30:27.64
To: "WRITING@ALBNYVMS.Bitnet"
Subj: RE: essay

Dave, I did get your message, and thank you. I will definately discuss the essay, you will hear from me soon. I am reviewing my text for background information.

From: ALBANY::WRITING 22-FEB-1995 17:16:29.91
To: "AW9999@ALBNYVMS.Bitnet"
Subj: RE: essay

Sounds good, Anne. You know where to find me when/if you're in the mood to talk... Good luck -- Dave

From: "AW9999@ALBNYVMS.BITNET" 27-FEB-1995 00:18:40.31
To: "writing@ALBNYVMS.Bitnet"
Subj: essay c/o dave coogan

Hi Dave, Here is the result of my first draft of my english essay. I am having trouble making my ideas connect. I feel like I am jumping all over the place. What do you think? How can I make my ideas connect and end with a solid conclusion? Most important do you think I answered the question?

Reading American Drama
Essay A9

Most notable among the plays "Winter's Night", Desire Under The Elms, Long Day's Journey Into Night, and The Little Foxes, was the explicit roles of men and women. The women were the keepers of the house, the men were keepers of the family. These roles had major impacts on the family structure. Eugene O'Neill's character, Abbie is rimarily concerned with having a "home." Being married is her ticket to living well.

By caring for her husband, who conveniently is old, she will gain his property when he dies. By having his last name, and cooking his meals, she gains what she never had. She will be financially secure. It is interesting that Ephriam continually puts Abbie in her place. Any reference Abbie makes to "my," and Ephriam claims that the property is his. Or he issues the label ours. Ephriam believes his wife's place is to care for the husband. In each of the plays the women have expected duties.

In Winter's Night, for example Rachel keeps a pretty house, and prepares a meal on the day of her husband's funeral, for her brother in-law. In one line she states "I shall wear my carpe a year for him, though heaven knows I've always hated black. I always did my duty by my husband." There is a suggestion that when a women marries it is her duty to keep house, feed and care for her husband, and ultimately bear his children.

Also present is the idea of the husband or a male being the provider. Both Ephriam and Eben exhibit a strong work ethic. Ephriam and Eben are always concerned with the upkeep of the farm. The farm is the key to financial prosperity. In Winter's Night, Jacob also ran a farm, and more importantly wants Rachel to remain in the role of a wife. He is incredulous that Rachel wants to make her own living. He wanted to provide for her. When he realizes that he can't have his notion of a family,he commits suicide.

What drives Jacob to suicide in part is his love for Rachel. Love is not the foundation of family in most of the plays. The noted exception is Awake and Sing, where Bessie does love her family, but she is so suffocating with that love, it leads to the break up of the family structure. Love is a secondary motive in the plays or it is the cause of the problems in the plays. For example, in Desire Under The Elms, Abbie marries for security. She doesn't love Ephriam. Regina, in The Little Foxes, also marries for security. She doesn't love her husband, she wants his money, and kills him when he interferes with her plans. Mary, in Long Day's Journey Into Night, has an addiction to morphine because she can't live up to her expected role as a wife and mother. She believes that the death of her first son was a result of her neglect. She feels her second son's weakness is also her fault, because she didn't provide for her sons. She believes she was happy before she was locked into the commitment of marriage. Marriage was a burdonsom duty. The plays have established the idea that women have secondary roles. The idea of femininity and weakness in terms of being dependent is also stressed. Mary is characterized as nervous, and pretty. "Her hair is arranged with fastidious care,her voice is soft and attractive." She consistently asks her husband and sons about her appearance. They must reassure her that she has never looked better.

Having the male figures in her life giving their approval seems to reaffirm her self worth. O'Neill displays similar characteristics in Abbie. She is also feminine and seductive. She uses her feminine charms to seduce Eben to give her the child that is key to giving her her ideas of home and security.

Themes of social mobility and respectability are also present in the family. Mary is constantly reprimanding her sons for drinking to much. Abbie also reprimands Eben for his liking of and taking pleasure from women. Such practices are seen as a disgrace to the family. In Long Day's Journey Into Night, Tyrone makes comments to his eldest son like "If you only had ambition in your head instead of folly!...You could still make your mark. You had the talent to become a fine actor! You have it still. You are my son!" The quote implies that because a child has their parents genes or blood, that they have the potential of achieving great things. The parents attempt to control their child's future. For example, in Desire under the elms, Ephriam calls his sons "natural born sinners" undeserving of his legacy of the farm. Ephriam believes them to be undeserving because they aren't as strong as he is. They are weak like their mother. Eben has to earn the right to run the farm, he isn't a natural air.

From: ALBANY::WRITING 27-FEB-1995 09:26:33.15
To: "AW9999@ALBNYVMS.Bitnet"
Subj: RE: essay c/o dave coogan

Anne,

Good job on the draft! It's coming along well. You certainly know the plays. Just reading through your draft, I get nice tight descriptions of each family and their gender roles. It's very accessible, especially for someone like me whose only seen Little Foxes.

I did want to ask you something, though --about these stereotypes of men and women. From the plays you discuss, do you think that the author (I guess, O'Neill) uses irony at all? I mean, are these stereotypical portraits of the woman as nurturer and the man as provider used without any awareness of their stereotypical status? My memory of the Little Foxes, was that Regina had some kind of feminist consciousness thing going --or a trace of it, anyway.

How would you characterize the way the author uses these stereotypes? (And by the way -- when is this paper due?)

Dave

From: "AW9999@ALBNYVMS.BITNET" 27-FEB-1995 11:30:24.08
To: "wRITING@ALBNYVMS.Bitnet"
Subj: RE: essay c/o dave coogan

Hi Dave, The essay is due tommorrow at 1:00. While I may have hit main points regarding the family structure, the prof. is famous for the line, you haven't flushed out your ideas enough. And I am terrible with conclusions I don't know how to wrap this up. As far as stereotypes the women may have feminist characterists but Regina specifically constrained by the time period. I think the thesis could be made stronger too. Any ideas? If I've answered the question, I guess it is time to fine tune. What do you think? Anne

---

From: ALBANY::WRITING 27-FEB-1995 18:38:55.34

To: "AW9999@ALBNYVMS.Bitnet"
Subj: RE: essay c/o dave coogan

Anne, I guess the reason I was asking about the playwrights' use of stereotypes, was to move us closer to a thesis. I felt like you answered the question in a general sense: you showed with numerous examples how women and men were portrayed. But what do you make of these portrayals? My question about how the writers used the stereotypes reveals one way of cracking the subject. But more generally, I might ask you, "Why do the authors create these portraits of the American family?" (you already discussed "how"....maybe now it's time to start thinking of why they did it? --Dave

---

From: "AW9999@ALBNYVMS.BITNET" 1-MAR-1995 22:57:14.16
To: "writing@ALBNYVMS.Bitnet"
Subj: essay results c/o Dave Coogan

Hi Dave, Remember the essay for my political science class? Well, I got a B. I was very pleased. Thanks again for your help. I've used the hot line quite a bit for writing and it seems like my writing improves each time. I was wondering if you have hours that you are in the writing center? You seem to pinpoint my weaknesses well. I'd like to continue to work with you if you are willing... I have another essay exam coming on the 8th. Would you mind helpin me out? Thanks. Anne .

p.s. I was trying to send you the final draft of my English essay. It was approximately six pages and the transfer was interrupted. Any idea why?

From: ALBANY::WRITING 3-MAR-1995 08:46:21.12
To: "AW9999@ALBNYVMS.Bitnet"
Subj: RE: essay results c/o Dave Coogan

Anne, Alright! You snagged a B....Way to go. I'm glad talking on e-mail helped. To answer your questions: I'd be happy to continue working with you on your essays. You can send stuff to WRITING (and mark it for me), or stop by the computer classroom and talk. Either way's fine with me.

About your file transfer? I don't know what happened. Could have been that you were trying to load a word processing file instead of an ASCII file. Hmmm.... Was that file you were trying to upload your final paper on the playwrights? -- Dave

---

From: "AW9999@ALBNYVMS.BITNET" 3-MAR-1995 12:50:35.62
To: "writing@ALBNYVMS.Bitnet"
Subj: essay c/o Dave Coogan

Well Dave, I don't know why it finally worked but here is the english essay as it was handed in. Minus the words that have no spaces in between them.... I don't understand computers at all. What do you think? Can we use this as a guide so I can write a better essay next time? Thanks as always. Anne

English 325
Reading American Drama
Essay A9

In the mid-1860s to 1900 people were raised primarily in an agricultural society. The year 1900 marked a change from a life that was agricultural to a life that was industrial. Plays like The Adding Machine are a clear criticism of that transition. Farmers became factory workers or worked in a business. Women left their domestic roles and became workers. Marriage and raising a family were postponed. People began to question roles that had always been accepted. Women in particular began to voice their opinions and broke to an extent their level of dependence on men. However, before the industrial growth, men and women had very specific roles. Women were in charge of the household, and having several children was common. The children were the inheritors of a legacy. They carried on the name and reputation of the family. It was important that a wife prepare her sons for their future roles as farmers, or bred winners. She also had to prepare her daughters for their role as a future wives and mothers. The male is dominant in the family. He is responsible for taking care of his wife and children. The male is key in the notion of free enterprise.

Having land meant future prosperity. That land and what was produced from it was the endowment to future generations. With the time came the expectations of high morality and a high work ethic. If a person didn't work hard and didn't produce, they were seen as failures. Drama expressed these ideals and the authors of the plays also cast characters in the constraints of the time.

Most notable among the plays "Winter's Night," Desire UnderThe Elms, Long Day's Journey Into Night, and The Little Foxes, was the explicit gender roles existing between men and women. The women were the keepers of the house, the men were keepers of the family. These differing roles had a major impact on the family structure. Women are depicted as dependent on men for stability and financial security. The woman is supposed to be grateful that she is being taken care of. She is supposed to be attentive to the needs of her husband and should happily fulfill those needs. Any assertion of individual identity or ownership is dismissed. For example, Eugene O'neill's character, Abbie is primarily concerned with having a "home." Being married is her ticket to living well. By caring for her old husband, she hopes she will gain his property when he dies. By having his last name, she hopes to gain what she never had. She wants to be financially secure. Ephriam continually puts Abbie in her place. Any reference Abbie makes to "my" house or property and Ephriam corrects her, claiming everything to be his. Or he issues the label of "ours." Ephriam believes that it is a woman's place is to care for the husband. In each of the plays women have expected duties.

In Winter's Night, Rachel keeps a pretty house, and prepares a meal on the day of her husband's funeral for her brother in-law. In one line she states "I shall wear my carpe a year for him, though heaven knows I've always hated black. I always did my duty by my husband." The quote suggests that when a woman gets married it is her duty is to keep house, feed and care for her husband, and ultimately bear his children. Also characteristic is the idea of the husband or the male figure being the provider. Both Ephriam and Eben exhibit a strong work ethic. Ephriam and Eben are always concerned with the up keep of the farm. The farm is the key to financial prosperity. In Winter's Night, Jacob also ran a farm, but he wants Rachel to remain in the role of a wife. He is incredulous to the idea of Rachel making her own living. He wanted to provide for her. When he realizes that he can't have his notion of a family, he commits suicide. What drives Jacob to suicide in part is his love for Rachel. Love is not the foundation of a family in most of the plays. The noted exceptions are the plays Awake and Sing and Long Day's Journey Into Night. However, the love is so suffocating with that it leads to the break up of the family structure. Love is a secondary motive in the plays or it is the cause of the problems in the plays. For example, in Desire Under The Elms, Abbie marries for security. She doesn't love Ephriam. Regina, in The Little Foxes, also marries for security. She doesn't love her husband, she wants his money, and kills him when he interferes with her plans.

The plays have established the idea that women have secondary roles. The ideas of femininity and weakness by being dependent are also stressed. A woman is supposed to make herself pretty, and follow the wishes of her husband. Mary is characterized as nervous, and pretty. "Her hair is arranged with fastidious care, her voice is soft and attractive." She consistently asks her husband and sons about her appearance. They must reassure her that she has never looked better. Having the male figures in her life giving their approval reaffirms herself worth. O'Neill displays similar characteristics in Abbie. She is also feminine and seductive. She uses her feminine charms to seduce Eben to give her the child that is key to gaining her ideals of having a home and security. Abbie will continue her duty as a wife, the only difference is that Abbie wants to please Eben instead of Ephriam.

Themes of social mobility and respectability are also present in the notion of family. Mary is constantly reprimanding her sons for drinking too much. Abbie also reprimands Eben for his liking of and taking pleasure from women. Such practices are seen as a disgrace to the family. In Long Day's Journey Into Night, Tyrone makes comments to his oldest son like "If you only had ambition in your head instead of folly!...You could still make your mark. You had the talent to become a fine actor! You have it still. You are my son! The quote implies that because a child has their parents genes, they have the potential of achieving great feats. The parents attempt to control their child's future. For example, in Desire Under The Elms, Ephriam calls his sons "natural born sinners" undeserving of his legacy of the farm. Ephriam believes them to be undeserving because they aren't as strong as he is. They are weak like their mother. Eben has to earn the right to run the farm, he isn't just a natural heir. A similar situation unfolds in Long Day's Journey Into Night. Referring to the earlier quote, Tyrone expects Jamie to carry on in his footsteps. Similarly, Ephriam wants Abbie to bear a son so his farm and land can be passed on, since his other sons are viewed as undeserving and incompetent to get the land.

Literature can be a reflection of the society and the time. Women were constrained in the period between 1865 and 1900. Women weren't allowed to vote, if they didn't marry who would take care of them? The idea that a man should provide for his wife is ingrained. Women were offered no alternative. Children were the product of their parents. They often took over the family farm or the family business. Qualities of reed and thrift came with the idea free enterprise. Men had to provide for the family.

There was often competition and worry that the family didn't look respectable in comparison to others. The danger that exists with the idea that a woman's place is in the home, or that a man is supposed to provide for his family, is that individuality and identity can be lost. Mary, in Long Day's Journey Into Night, has an addiction to morphine because she can't live up to her expected role as a wife and mother. She believes that the death of her first son was a result of her neglect. She believes that her second son's weakness is also her fault because she didn't provide for her sons. She believes she was happy before she was locked into the commitment of marriage. Marriage was a burdensome duty. Eben and Abbie lose everything important to them because they try to fit the stereotypical role. Abbie sees marriage as her key to financial reward and Eben is also caught up in the wealth and success the farm can bring.

The portrait of the family in the mid 1860's to 1900 became an ideal that people tried to hold on to in a changing society. Women are now in the working world, but they earn approximately sixty cents on every dollar a man makes in a day. The thought process still appears to be the same. A woman can work, but she still is expected to tend to her family. Men are still dominant in business. According to society men should still be the providers. This of course is not considering the single parent. Children still carry on the family name. They are expected to achieve if not better their parent's level success. At the very least, there is the pressure to achieve or better that success. Is this the kind of legacy we want to leave other generations in the twenty-first century? I hope not.

From: ALBANY::WRITING 7-MAR-1995 15:44:32.90
To: "AW9999@ALBNYVMS.Bitnet"
Subj: RE: essay c/o Dave Coogan

Anne,

Sorry to be getting back to you so late. I finally got a chance to read the revision, and (wow!)... you really sharpened the focus here! You went from a catalog of incidents from the plays to contextualizing the plays (and their portraits of the family) within history.

Another strong point in this draft is the way you explain the quotes you use. Having not read the plays, I rely on your explanations to make sense of them. And I found these explanations to be very succint and clear.

I do think we can use this essay, and the earlier draft, to work on your writing. It seems like the major change from the draft to the final version is in the way you create your theme. I noticed that you did this primarily by writing an introduction and a conclusion around the body of your paper. In a sense, you trust yourself to intuit your meaning while you're drafting, but then you benefit from a little distance, or some conversation, or simply some time away from the draft, where you can figure out exactly what it is you're arguing. Does this make sense? I'm trying to figure out your writing process so you can repeat it in the future.

There was one more thing I wanted to talk about. Actually, two more things. The first is that I'm still not convinced that these representations of the characters are to be taken at face value. I mean, the way you present the characters, they are helping you prove your points, I know. But is this all there is in the play? (Maybe I'm just amazed that such plays could exist: could they really be that unreflective about the gender roles they are offering?)

I want to extend this last point to your overall tone in the paper. What I heard was a mixture of empathetic argument (you feel sorry for these women who did not have their independence) and naivity. Do you think all women really just accepted that lifestyle? There may be a geographical thing going on here: I heard once that some women from the east coast (during the mid 1800s) wanted to move out west in order to find independence. They didn't want the city life, the social pressures. Also, (and I admit this may be tangentially related as well) Louisa May Alcott's _Little Women_ appears to be more critical of that stereotyped woman's role as wife/mother. Have you seen that movie (or read that book?)

These are just some thoughts for you. (I hadn't intended to write this much. I was going to try and point the spots in the text where these issues came up. But this seems ok for now.) We're just getting started, anyway. So I invite you to think more about the way you write your papers, the issues you raise in this paper, and of course your own questions as we continue this dialogue.

Talk to you soon, Dave

From: "AW9999@ALBNYVMS.BITNET" 7-MAR-1995 16:43:53.03
To: "WRITING@ALBNYVMS.Bitnet"
Subj: RE: essay c/o Dave Coogan

Thank you for reading over the essay Dave. I think that you made some very valid points. It will be interesting when I get the paper back with the comments, she could bring up the same things. As far as the overall tone to the paper, my main point (hopefully) was that women were constrained within that time period. And I don't think that women in life accepted the roles handed to them. Women as portrayed within literature did. (At least, the works in class did. Case exception: The Little Foxes.)

[See Note 2]
ahh, see this is very interesting to me —the way you phrase it. "I don't think that women in life accepted the roles handed to them. Women in literature did." This raises

intriguing questions to me about who these authors were, and how their view of the family fits in with (or somehow misrepresents) what real women did. You suggest that things were different in real life: I tend to agree. But how might we prove this? Are there any testimonials from the time? perhaps revisionary histories of the 19th century?

You might be interested in the fact that I used the paper as a basis for my feminism class. Though I don't agree with many feminist view points.... I'll send that if you like. (I think I will.)

Yes, by all means send it.

Also when the pressure from midterms die, I'd like to discuss my test essays with you.

---

ok.

I had the complaint that I didn't explain both sides of the issue in enough detail. (The sides being Federalist and Anti Federalist) I may benefit from distance I am not sure but when you have a time constraint of 50 minutes or an hour, that doesn't cut it.

Yes. The essay test is a whole different genre from the five page or ten page paper. Distance is hard to come by when you're on the clock. But perhaps this critique you received has something to do with my earlier comment about your reading of the plays. There is a feeling I get when I read your stuff that you take a lot of what you're dealing with at face value. You portray the 19th century in pretty absolutist terms in your paper. But when I ask you if you think all women accpeted this status, you write back and say no. Soooooooooooooooooo, either I misread your essay (or read it too quickly?), or there's something we need to work on? Irony? Street-saavy? or maybe just critical reflection? Not sure yet. I may have to read some more of your stuff to figure it out. Though it occurs to me you may have some ideas!

From: "AW9999@ALBNYVMS.BITNET" 8-MAR-1995 09:20:56.62
To: "WRITING@ALBNYVMS.Bitnet"

Good Morning Dave,

In that essay when you say I take things at face value, I do. I don't think that you misread the piece, I was working with how I read the play. When you say critical reflection, do you mean that I don't put enough of my opinion in the piece?

Yes, that's the idea. More opinion. But not at the expense of that rich context you provide (!) In other words, I think there's a way that you can use those quotes and those summaries of scenes that you do so well to prove a larger point. This is what I mean by critical reflection: using the text to your advantage. Use it, instead of reproducing it. Make it fit your needs. I think this, more than anything else, is what gives writers authority, and yes --this posture would characterize the kind of writing done in upper level classes.

Another thought, how might you determine the authors perspective if an outside source is not required and there is a time constraint for research? I am not saying that I wouldn't do the research...

Same issue. I'm trying to think of this posture in a physical way. It's the difference between leaning back while you read and hunching forward, into the text. I think of it as trying to read between the lines, or to see through the page. This activity doesn't always require research. (sometimes, just a lot of gall!)

Another thing I thought about. There are different types of writing, for let's say English and poly sci. In what ways do they differ?

Ahh. Yes. They are different and they are the same. Different in that they have distinct disciplinary concerns, different ways of using writing. But the same, because they come from you. It's all your writing.

I guess what I am saying is I don't feel like I'm meeting the criteria... i.e. I don't explain enough or give enough detail... What do you think?

I think you're being too hard on yourself :-}

I'll send the other paper later today. Thanks for following up with me. I think I'm going to learn a lot from you. Anne

From: ALBANY::WRITING 9-MAR-1995 16:20:20.46
To: "AW9999@ALBNYVMS.Bitnet"
Subj: RE: essay c/o Dave Coogan

Anne--I received your essay from your feminism class, and plan to take a look at it sometime tomorrow. Will you be here over spring break? If so, I thought we could continue this conversation. If not, I'd just as soon take some more time to read you essay. (Let me know your plans...)--Dave

From:"AW9999@ALBNYVMS.BITNET" 9-MAR-1995 18:41:55.14
To: "WRITING@ALBNYVMS.Bitnet"
Subj: RE: essay c/o Dave Coogan

Hi Dave, From your message I am under the impression that you are a graduate student? I won't be here over the break. I will be in Florida until the 19th. I got the english essay back and got a B on the paper. Next time I want it to be an A. Proffesor B.'s comments were the following:

"Anne-You've got the material for a book here, but rather too much for an essay. You've got a fine grasp of how these women are hampered by lack of a financial power, the often necessarily mercenary reasons they marry. You also make many good observations about parents amd children. The problem is that you try to cover to much-- a half dozen plays, nearly every concievable family relationship-- that you don't get into explore one in depth. The essay frame is intriguing, but I am not sure how it relates to the plays themselves. On which historical period are you focusing? Long Day's Journey is set in 1912. After industrialization but Desire under the Elms takes place in 1850's. Does this have any effect on how women/ families are portrayed? (I thought this was the base for my argument!) You start to make an important point about Ephriam, that he cares more about money, than providing love and offering protection to his family but you suddenly switch (I think that word is the key or start anyway to the problem...) switch to Jacob's suicide. You are surely right that the females marry for economic security, but what about men? Why do they marry? Can they unlike most of the women afford to look for someone love or to whom they are sexually attracted? Don't be afraid to narrow your focus to a few important issues and give your good ideas (this is a recording) the full discussion they merit."

Okay, in my writing can you see what she means? I'm not sure that I do exactly. I have a feeling that from what I have sent you and from comments said, the problem is the same. After break I'd like to go through this paper (perhaps in person) with you. The problem with meeting in person is my schedule. Are you available ever Mondays, 9:00-12. (Wednesday's and Friday's same time.) Also I still would like to go through the test essays. I get the public affairs back tomorrow. So, I may type it up and send it along.

Just in response, to "I think you are too hard on yourself." Always, I want to put my best work forward, and reach my highest potential. So far, I don't think that is happening... That's why I came to you for help. I also brought up the question about the different kinds of writing because I feel the same weakness coming up in my other classes. I'd like to get my writing up to par/speed for those classes. I look forward to hearing your thoughts. Have a nice break. Anne.

It is hard not to admire Anne's dogged determination throughout this process. Her honesty, in the face of her own ignorance, however, is not just inspiring but disquieting, because her need to "meet the criteria" does not so much validate the criteria, in my view, as it calls into question the value of the criteria. Her difficulty is that she seems to be unaware of what Geisler (1994) calls the problem space of rhetorical process. Consider, for example, the following sentences, taken from the beginning and the end of her second draft.

> Drama expressed these ideals and the authors of the plays also cast characters in the constraints of the time.

> The portrait of the family in the mid 1860's to 1900 became an ideal that people tried to hold on to in a changing society.

What's interesting here is the way the responsibility for gender-identity shifts, tentatively, from authors to reality. What begins as a discussion of the plays ends as a discussion of history—a presentation of "how things were" based, primarily, it would seem, upon a reading of literature. In the first sentence, for example, responsibility is shared: Drama may have merely "expressed these ideals" of family life but authors also "cast characters in the constraints of the time." But in the second sentence, which comes during the conclusion, these qualifications are no longer made. The portrait of the family becomes autonomous, something "that people" not authors "tried to hold up." Although the body of her paper does, in fact, detail the ways in which the plays constructed family life around rigid expectations of male/female roles, her understanding of these roles as rhetorical constructions remains elusive. She talks about the plays but not about the authors. Thus, as a writer of literary criticism, Anne tends to stick to what Geisler calls the problem space of domain content. As she sees it, her task is to get the facts straight.

Anne's parenthetical dialogue with her English professor is instructive in this regard. In this message, where she talks back to the professor's end comments, she transforms the professors' comments about rhetoric into comments about content. For example, when the professor asks her how the different time frames for each play might alter "the" portrait of the American family, Anne only hears this negatively, as the professor's gross mis-understanding of her intentions: "I thought this [the portrayal of women and families] was the base for my argument!" However, when the professor accuses Anne of making sudden switches in her argument, she does not resist the critique: "I think that word [switch] is the key or start anyway to the problem." The issue, here, is that she switches between different sets of facts too rapidly, without controlling the process. To control the process, however, she needs to control much more than the domain content. "I had the complaint," says Anne about her political science test, "that I didn't explain both sides of the issue in enough detail." In my response, I validate the critique, suggesting along the way that perhaps "you take too much at face value." To Anne, however, the issue is more cut and dry: "I guess what I'm saying is I don't feel like I'm meeting the criteria." When I complicate this conclusion with the idea of critical reflection, Anne construes this as an opposition to criteria: "Do you mean that I don't put enough of my own opinion into the piece?"

This choice of words, familiar to practitioners and theorists alike, is important to highlight because it so plainly re-asserts the divide between experts and novices, placing Anne on the novice side—skeptical, as any novice would be, of her own opinion. According to Geisler (1994), it is an unremarkable distinction for both teachers and students, because "at no part in the cycle of school literacy do either teachers or students routinely expect to see knowledge transforming in students' texts. Indeed, regulated by the idea of the autonomous text, students early on are asked to stay as close to the source texts as possible" (p. 51). Anne is right, strictly speaking then, to distrust the value of her opinion. It is not clear to me, however, that this should be the case, either for Anne or for other students; not clear that the distinction between facts and opinion is a distinction worth defending, or more precisely, that the struggle between naiveté and academic gamesmanship, lay knowledge and expert knowledge, is a struggle worth pursuing in the electronic writing center.

In foregrounding the ways in which email cannot change these dynamics of literacy, I don't mean to imply that email changed nothing. Much like the other students that I discussed in the last chapter, Anne also used email to seek out an internally persuasive discourse, albeit in more limited ways. For example, in response to my skeptical reading of her paper, Anne shot back, "I don't think that women in life accepted the roles handed to them. Women as portrayed in literature did." The diction of the above-quoted passage, much like the diction of Katie and Bill's email, suggests an exigency for communication not present in the formal writing task: In the heat of informal, written dialogue, these students end up saying things that they would not—perhaps, could not—say in their written monologues. As a dialogic writing partner, then, Anne appears more willing to consider alternatives to the idea that literature simply represents reality. But this willingness is overwhelmed by an (understandable) anxiety to answer the hail of the ISA; to be the writer she is supposed to be in both English and Political Science classes.

Even when disciplinarity is not so obviously at stake, the pressure to respond to the ISA remains, as one can tell from the subject line of the following session. This student, a non-native speaker of English, perhaps perceives that ISA differently than Anne, but he perceives it just the same.

From: ALBANY::L1234 26-APR-1993 20:15:31.07
To: WRITING
Subj   :Kee, for his 130 class, letter form about rural and urban life in 16th century Europe. Please check if make sense and any grammatical errors. thanks

Martin Guerre to Balthasar, Sr
1584 in Artigat.
Honest, friendly, dear friend.

Congratulation! My old friend. May God will bring thousand happiness to your son and his bride; Balthasar & Magdalena's wedding, and to your household. My good man, time really past us very fast. It seems like within the time of a wink, our sons and daughters had grown and ready for marriage.

I think our new generation is more lucky than we are, and if God would give me a second chance to choose; I think I will rather be a merchant, living in urban, much the same like Balthasar & Magdalena, because in the urban there are more things going on, like carnivals, fairs, and etc... The transportation network is so large, which make business, traveling, and communication more convenience.

Although there are inflation, but I believe the increase in population especially in the rural, and commerce will balance it out. In other words there are more customers in the market, whom I can make money from them. The life of an enterpriser is always easier, than a hard life peasant working with long hours works, and depend our income on the weather. It is true that the price of agricultural product rose the most, but I rather be a bourgeoisie enjoying my liberties. For example, even Magdalena can travel and become the helper of Balthasar. They both are more or less educated, or trying to improve their knowledge by exposing themselves to the knowledge around them. They trust and respect each other, they share everything, they wrote letters periodically to keep their long distance relationship steady. It is not my fault, it is neither my wife's fault, it is the fault of our society, that made us separated and suffered for fifteen years. I notice there is really no difference for us to separate, because I hardly communicate with her as much as my ancestors did to their wives. I think it is what made Arnaud duTilh impersonated me for three years possible. The love between I and Bertrande is so shallow, that we are like strangers, only know each other from the outside, and never the inside.

In the rural we have kids, because we want more helping hands to work on the field, and never put emotion to them. Simply, there is not a person like Magdalena, who hook up everyone within and out of the family for domestic and business purposes. I think it is the major factor that lead middle classes to become economically succeed as the aristocrat. It is also possible to raise status by intermarrying with the aristocrat from the middle class, where it is not likely for peasants to do so.

If you ask me why I didn't leave Artigat for Nuremberg, I can tell you that, I can't leave my family, my country, my people again. Selling all my ancestral property in Hendaye, leaving my ancestral tomb, losing my mother tongue! Just for liberties?! I think it is not enough to make me go. I think it will be too radical for me to go. I didn't choose my life, but I choose how to manage my life. I manage it after God had chosen it for me. I believe he see this life fits me best. I believe justice is the name of my Lord, therefore all my suffering will soon pays off in after life. I hope you will forgive me by being so angry. I think you will understand and agree with me. Anyway, it is always a lost if I can no longer sell you crops to distribute in Germany. Right? I know I shouldn't be complaining, because there are thousands and millions of people suffer more than I do. For example the serfdom in Russia, the hereditary subjection in Germany. It becomes less civilized as you go from west in Europe to the east, but there is not much political and religious difference in France and Germany Nowadays. At least we are becoming small proprietors. I know one day we will gain as much liberties as the German urban here in France.

Do you remember the year 1556 the year we part? There are a lot of changes that have been made by Europe. Before 1548 I was 24 and was fought in the Spanish force under the same king of Germany; Charles the fifth against Francis the first of France joined with Turks alliance. In 1547, Henry the second of France taking Francis the first's place & joining the League of Schmalkald against us. After seven years of religious war the Peace of Augsburg had settled it in 1555, and the year after it, Philip the second of Spain tool all the holdings west of France from Charles the Fifth. There I retreated along with them. Oh, I am sorry if I bore you again. I am just like history repeating my self again, just like the Wars of Religion in Germany was fighting in France now.

Maybe I shouldn't be so stubborn, or I am getting too old for politic. I am now 60 years old. I know I will not live long. It is the main reason, that I wrote you this letter, because I am not afraid of commiting treason. If I am I wouldn't come back to France 36 year ago.

Nowadays, there is really no one worth while to trust around here when it comes to religion. I believe you will not tell anyone, that I have discuss my second thoughts about Catholic, because I know you are a good Protestant. I believe everything is divinity and predestine, therefore I am not afraid of being caught, because if God wants to call me back to him, he would made me hanged for treason, or died in the war some 36 years ago. Faith alone will lead us to do good, just as God wants us to be, therefore possessing the grace of God by speak no evil or not saying anything against Catholic thinking, see no evil or never lay an eye on a censored book, and hear no evil from the new protestant ideas. It will do us no good, because these only prevent us from communicate, and improve our progress. They are just covering up the truth, and want us to remain in their, "bread and Circus." game.

In 1562 our civil war begins, which is the year I am back to France. War of Religion had held in France for 22 years already, and it is still going on. The death of Henry the second of France had made our monarchy and nation even weaker. The power had fallen onto the hands of the aristocrat. These lead to political and religious disunity within a certain large France.

We are divided just like the German state, each with its own laws, parliament and etc..., the most important difference between us is German religious right are protected by the Peace of Augsburg, and we have no such document to protect our religious rights, yet.

My good man, I have nothing to say. I am here to send you thousands of blessings in the name of the Lord to you and your family and friends. I am blessing good health and wealth to the newly marry couple; Magdalena & Balthasar. May God give them a son soon.

Honest, truthful, friendly
Martin Guerre.

From: ALBANY::WRITING 26-APR-1993 20:34:52.51
To: ALBANY::L1234
Subj: RE: Kee, for his 130 class, letter form about rural and urban life in 16th century Europe. Please check if make sense and any grammatical errors. thanks

Kee: I received your paper and have begun to read it but I'm curious -- what was the assignment? And what is the name of the class you are writing the paper for? --Dave

---

From: ALBANY::L1234 26-APR-1993 20:45:25.63
To: ALBANY::WRITING
Subj: RE: Kee, for his 130 class, letter form about rural and urban life in 16th century Europe. Please check if make sense and any grammatical errors. thanks

I am writing a paper for my European civilization I class. It's about rural and urban living in 16th century Europe. Its based on Magdalena & Balthasar and The return of Martin Guerre. The Protestant Reformation has taken place.

From: ALBANY::L1234 26-APR-1993 21:31:07.99
To: ALBANY::WRITING
Subj: RE: Kee, for his 130 class, letter form about rural and urban life in 16th century Europe. Please check if make sense and any grammatical errors. thanks

Magdalena and Balthasar is the name of a book, which is about the middle class couple, Magdalena is the wife and Balthasar is the hudsband, who always travel and do family businesses in amoung the German Protestant states. Martin is a peasant, who ran away to escape being caught stealing. after his father died he is forgiven for stealing within his family and became the only heir to his family holdings. but someone came back and impersonated him for 3 years and Martin was back to France again and claimed his identity. Here I am relating these two stories by writing in a letter form from Martin to Balthasar's father.

From: ALBANY::WRITING 26-APR-1993 21:45:27.89
To: ALBANY::L1234
Subj: RE: Kee, for his 130 class, letter form about rural and urban life in 16th century
Europe. Please check if make sense and any grammatical errors. thanks

Kee: I think I'm starting to get a handle on this stuff. But to be honest with you, I
understood more about the topic from your note to me than from the letter (the actual
assignment). In fact, your English was better in the note to me than it was in the letter.
Try relating the story to me, right now. That would help me with the context and help
me figure out why Martin would have any reason to write a letter to Balthasar. Is this a
letter of apology? A retropsect of their time together? --Dave

---

From: ALBANY::L1234 26-APR-1993 21:59:08.50
To: ALBANY::WRITING
Subj: RE: Kee, for his 130 class, letter form about rural and urban life in 16th century
Europe. Please check if make sense and any grammatical errors. thanks

after Martin left his family he went to spain the fifth is the king of Germany and Spain
therefore he was send to fought in Germany to against France his own country. There I
carry the story and make Martin meet Balthasar's father.

In order to introduce the life of 16th century Europe, I let Martin writing this letter to
his friend Balthasar's father. In the letter I disscuss the events of both country (France
& Germany) that had happened. It also introduce how dangerous it is to talk back or
give opinion of Catholic church in France during the War of Religion (another case of
Catholic VS.protestant). It is not a letter of apology, but a more like a private talk or a
dairy writing.

From: ALBANY::WRITING 26-APR-1993 22:30:04.24
To: ALBANY::L1234
Subj: RE: Kee, for his 130 class, letter form about rural and urban life in 16th century
Europe. Please check if make sense and any grammatical errors. thanks

Kee: I'm starting to sense a tension in your paper --a tension between the changing
economic scene and religious politics. In one spot you say (or rather, Martin says) I
did not choose my life --God did. And throughout the letter I sense Martin has a very
strong faith. But I also sense that
Martin believes the economy also determines who he is --he said that if he had it to do
all over again, he'd be a merchant. Why is this? Why does he want to enjoy the

"liberties" of the bourgoise? Does he think that sort of life would have improved his relationship with his wife? Does he think God would have willed this life on him? --Dave

---

From: ALBANY::L1234 26-APR-1993 22:39:45.40
To: ALBANY::WRITING
Subj: RE: Kee, for his 130 class, letter form about rural and urban life in 16th century Europe. Please check if make sense and any grammatical errors. thanks

because Martin's life is just full of unhappiness, therefore it is really a complain, but he know it is God who willed this life on him. Therefore he will do his best to recieve what God gives him. He know God is always right and he knows his sufferings will soon pay off. Even though, he is a loser. He is jeolous, but he does't admit it, because a good christian shouldn't be so.

From: ALBANY::WRITING 26-APR-1993 23:03:08.75
To: ALBANY::L1234
Subj: RE: Kee, for his 130 class, letter form about rural and urban life in 16th century Europe. Please check if make sense and any grammatical errors. thanks

yeah, but don't you think Martin is also a victim of the political and economic conditions of his generation? Or is it all God's fault?

From: ALBANY::L1234 27-APR-1993 23:53:53.66
To: ALBANY::WRITING
Subj: RE: Kee, for his 130 class, letter form about rural and urban life in 16th century Europe. Please check if make sense and any grammatical errors. thanks

in times of trouble. Thanks...

From: ALBANY::WRITING 28-APR-1993 22:00:01.71
To: ALBANY::L1234
Subj: RE: Kee, for his 130 class, letter form about rural and urban life in 16th century Europe. Please check if make sense and any grammatical errors. thanks

You're quite welcome, Kee. --Dave

From: ALBANY::L1234 3-MAY-1993 15:28:18.07
To: ALBANY::WRITING
Subj: RE: Kee, for his 130 class, letter form about rural and urban life in 16th century
Europe. Please check if make sense and any grammatical errors. thanks

Dave: This is Kee, I sent you the paper days ago, I am a little curious about the paper.
Did you finish checking it? Have you make any other comments? How can I get an
answer? Are you going to reply soon with the final paper?

From: ALBANY::WRITING 3-MAY-1993 15:50:56.32
To: ALBANY::L1234
Subj: RE: Kee, for his 130 class, letter form about rural and urban life in 16th century
Europe. Please check if make sense and any grammatical errors. thanks

Kee: I must have misinterpretted your last message (oops). When you said, "in times
of trouble, Thanks" I assumed you had gotten all you wanted from WRITING. What
else would you like to talk about? (Or rather, what do you want me to talk about?)
--Dave

This session is interesting, in part, because of the spectacular mis-
understanding. What I had construed as the tutorial, itself—the email we ex-
changed about the purpose of the letter, the thoughts of the main character, and the
context of this historical period—Kee had construed as nothing more than the
obligatory giving of details, the prologue before the main attraction. It is tempting,
then, to conclude right away that the reason why this session does not work is that it
fails, in Kee's words, to "make sense" of the English. It does not reach the main attraction. That conclusion, however, is not completely satisfying. What Kee needs is
not so much advice on syntax and grammar—or not just that kind of advice—but a
point of view on using English in the context of this history class.

Yet this is not what Kee asks for. When he sees the writing center, Kee does not see
an invitation to think and write like a historian, much less an opportunity to dialogize his
thinking. He sees an authoritative discourse or "grammar" to be mastered. It is entirely
understandable. As Bakhtin (1981) reminds us, centripetal discourse always "makes its
real presence felt" by "imposing specific limits" on the language of heteroglossia until
it creates a "firm, stable linguistic nucleus" (p. 271). And while it is tempting, perhaps,
to dismiss the relevance of Bakhtin's work in this context—he was, after all, discussing
Russian literary discourse not Edited American English (EAE)—I believe the work is
relevant because it helps us understand the tension that writers like Kee face when they
try to complete their assignments in the writing center.

Bakhtin has argued that "every utterance participates in the 'unitary language'
(in its centripetal forces and tendencies) and at the same time partakes of social and

historical heteroglossia (the centrifugal, stratifying forces)" (p. 272). Discourse, he seems to say, is Janus-faced, with one eye on the centripetal and one eye on the centrifugal. "It is possible," then, according to Bakhtin, "to give a concrete and detailed analysis of any utterance, once having exposed it as a contradiction-ridden, tension-filled unity of two embattled tendencies in the life of language" (p. 272). What I take this to mean is that a person's gesture toward centripetal discourse can always be interpreted differently as a movement away from centrifugal discourse. Susan Miller (1989), perhaps, has a similar point in mind when she notes that "writers are always deciding to make a statement, within oscillating powers that simultaneously impel and retard the decision" (p. 20). She reminds us that every fiction of textual presence conceals a centrifugal voicing or two.

If we look again at Kee's assignment, and we think about Kee not as a traditional author, per se, but as the author of a historical persona (Martin Guerre), we can expand what we think of as his dilemma to "make sense." As well, if we look beyond Kee's dissonance within the standards of EAE, we see a much more profound type of dissonance in his thinking. In the assignment, Kee is asked "to introduce the life of 16th century Europe" by having his central character engage in a "private talk or a dairy [sic] writing." Whether he chose this genre or it was chosen for him, the situation raises interesting questions about Kee's relationships to Martin Guerre and academic history. Consider, for example, the following passage.

> Do you remember the year 1556 the year we part? There are a lot of changes that have been made by Europe. Before 1548 I was 24 and was fought in the Spanish force under the same king of Germany; Charles the fifth against Francis the first of France joined with Turks alliance. In 1547, Henry the second of France taking Francis the first's place & joining the League of Schmalkald against us. After seven years of religious war the Peace of Augsburg had settled it in 1555, and the year after it, Philip the second of Spain tool all the holdings west of France from Charles the Fifth. There I retreated along with them. Oh, I am sorry if I bore you again. I am just like history repeating my self again, just like the Wars of Religion in Germany was fighting in France now.

According to Bakhtin (1990), the central task in the creation of a literary character is to "become another in relation" to oneself. But what does Kee become in this passage? Does he become a historian—the scholar of 16th century European life? Or does he become the peasant farmer complaining about the ways in which his life has changed? It would seem that he becomes neither. Apparently, the point of his opening question is not really to inquire about Balthassar's memory of 1556, but to give Kee a chance to display his knowledge of war history. It seems likely, then, that this is not done to impress Balthassar but to impress the teacher. While it is true that Kee does insert his character into the story, the insertion does not fundamentally change the way in which we are asked to read the passage. In fact, the bulk of it becomes a kind of short-hand or class-notes history—"Charles the fifth against Francis the first of France" and so on, as if history were just a litany of names. At the end of the passage, then, Kee-the-student becomes Kee-the-character, addressing Balthassar in a more casual way: "Oh, I am sorry if I bore you again." Yet this brief flirtation with the character of Martin Guerre is over before it begins: "I am just like history repeating myself again just like the Wars of Religion in Germany . . . "

To Bakhtin (1990), of course, it is natural for writers, in the process of creating a character to experience these tensions: "Before the countenance of the hero finally takes shape as a stable and necessary whole, the hero is going to exhibit a great many grimaces, random masks, wrong gestures, and unexpected actions" (p. 6). Martin Guerre, Kee's "hero", indeed makes a great many unexpected moves in the letter, which only remind us of how difficult it is for him to sustain the fiction that he is in control. Here, for example, is Kee on the subject of class: "It is also possible to raise status by intermarrying with the aristocrat from the middle class, where it is not likely for peasants to do so." As Bartholomae (1985) suggests, "such sentences fall apart not because the writer lacks the necessary syntax to glue the pieces together but because he lacks the full statement within which these key words are already operating." (p. 284). Would Martin use words like middle class? (Did the phrase even exist then?)

While email tutoring, theoretically, opens up a range of centrifugal discourses, this session is characterized, more often than not, by Kee's attempts to control what Bartholomae calls the "full statement" of history.

What needs to be controlled, in Bartholomae's view, however, are not just discourse conventions but "political and social relationships" (p. 277) between the writer and the audience. Part of that relationship, for a non-native speaker, has to do with EAE. My larger point, though, is that when Kee loses control of that centripetal discourse, he gains the centrifugal discourse of his character, Martin Guerre, as evidenced in this passage: "If you ask me why I didn't leave Artigat for Nuremberg, I can tell you that, I can't leave my family, my country, my people again. Selling all my ancestral property in Hendaye, leaving my ancestral tomb, losing my mother tongue! Just for liberties?!" Sentences like these, admittedly not perfect, nevertheless stand out from the others as powerful voicings of the subject matter. They also suggest that there are other ways to "do history" or control the "full statement" of history in college writing; that the learning of history need not be linked absolutely with the learning of disciplinary genres or the mastery of EAE.

As well, these sentences suggest that the strong, forceful diction that I praised as centrifugal discourse, in the previous chapter, is not dependent upon email but upon dialogue. In this case, the sentences were not written in dialogue with me but in dialogue with Balthassar. Bartholomae's main point about this kind of assignment, however, bears further comment. To Bartholomae, the real challenge in college writing lies in producing the "fiction" of an academic language, "a language," he believes the students "are aware of but cannot control" (p. 276). Having students write to someone other than the teacher, he argues, is ultimately misleading because it denies "the situation of the classroom" (p. 277). The central problem of academic writing, he says, is the problem "of being granted a special right to speak" (p. 278).

To him, that right is not earned through originality but through conventionality, or a process of learning the commonplaces that academics value. It is easy to see where Kee struggles with these commonplaces throughout the letter. But I am less certain than Bartholomae, perhaps, that this struggle is worth defending. Maybe the professor of this 100 level history course agrees. Maybe that is why he or she created the assignment?

Although I believe in helping students appropriate disciplinary discourse, especially in their majors, and I believe in helping non-native speakers learn EAE, I want to contest the notion that the only source of power worth pursuing in writing is the power of EAE and of academic discourse. What would have happened, for example, if instead of a tutorial response, I had sent Kee a letter, written in the character of Balthassar? Can we imagine a dialogized space in the writing center where students "do history" outside the gaze of centripetal discourse? It seems to me that such a space would contradict what the academy stands for. Yet I don't know why such a contradiction would need to be quelled. If the point of undergraduate education, particularly in the "gen-ed" sequence, is to engage new subjects and employ them in the service of local needs and current interests of both faculty, students, and other communities, then I feel we need more nimble forms of collaborative writing, which emphasize power *between* two or more people who have become answerable to each other. If, however, the point of undergraduate education is to inculcate in students a respect for expertise, preserve the autonomy of the writer, and sustain the Strategy of Containment, then we should abandon dialogic literacy as an irresponsible movement away from existing modes of power-in-writing.

IF THE MEDIUM IS NOT THE MESSAGE, THEN WHAT IS?

Obviously, or so it seems to me as I contemplate these sessions, the presence of email in a writing center does not produce dialogic literacy anymore than the presence of a blackboard in a classroom produces a lecture. In fact, email may do very little to change perceptions of the writing center. To create new forums for dialogic literacy, we will need much more than computers but a refigured ISA of literacy. My point, finally, is not that email changes nothing—that it is just a transparent window on the conference, revealing problems that already exist. Nor is my point that email changes everything. The point is this: Should we decide to do nothing innovative in the center with new technologies such as email, nothing will occur.

In the next chapter, I make a modest proposal to reframe this dilemma by defining and then illustrating the idea of an electronic writing center—that larger, conceptual, electronic space that sponsors, among other things, dialogic, email tutorials. The distinction I am making between an electronic writing center (EWC) and an online writing lab (OWL) is not merely semantic. An OWL typically uses the Internet to distribute information to writers about grammar, style, genre, and the composing process. OWLs can also become launch-pads to Internet search engines, online library catalogs, dictionaries, subject guides (Humanities, Social Sciences, etc.), and other online writing labs (OWLs). In most cases, OWLs perpetuate what Andrea Lunsford (1991) has called the "storehouse" version of the writing center—a large warehouse filled with knowledge about writing. In storehouse centers, knowledge is "immediately accessible, individually knowable, measurable, and shareable" (p. 4), it is exterior to the self, and exists independently of human perception. Students who interact with OWLs are implicitly asked to see knowledge about writing as something "on the web."

Although online tutoring services have been integrated into many of these OWLs, most directors report that interest in this service pales in comparison to the interest in face-to-face tutoring. The reasons, however, go beyond the problems of equitable access to technology and the pedagogical concern for shared space, though these are serious issues. In fact, the lack of interest in full-scale, online conferences, both by tutors and students, seems directly related to the popularity of electronic storehouse centers. Although these services make sophisticated use of new computer technologies, their main innovation, upon closer inspection does not appear to be technical, or even theoretical, but political. Storehouse centers, whether they take shape in physical reality or virtual reality, are easily assimilated into the academic community because they are the least disruptive of the status quo: They please those members of the academic community determined to reassert functionalism, and they please traditional writing centers because they in no way promise to teach the more humane aspects of the writing process: web pages are not teaching machines, and they are certainly not conferences.

Although this adaptation of the Internet is politic, it is, in my view, not a means to an end but an end in itself—and not a very promising one, at that. By using the internet to entrench the Strategy of Containment and the Rhetoric of Technocentrism, writing centers may be subverting their own, often explicitly stated desire to be associated with something other than functional literacy. OWLs, after all, are not built in order to open up what Bakhtin calls the centrifugal aspects of discourse. Rather, it is the other way around. The academy allows OWLs, computer labs, and writing centers to exist so long as they promise to improve writing skills or take care of writing problems—to re-assert the centripetal aspects of discourse. Against this Rhetoric of Technocentrism, which would only re-assert the hail of functional literacy online, I propose an electronic space that expands the concept of audience, deprivatizes the writing tutorial, and makes innovative use of other students' writings. Instead of rebuilding the containment zone online, we should be developing electronic contact zones.

If, however, we find that more students and faculty want electronic spaces to clean up grammar in finished texts, or to look up facts about writing, we can at least understand this situation for what it is: the ISA of functional literacy reproducing itself by controlling the latest relations of production in cyberspace. Clearly, these relations of production that create new electronic environments are not "out there" anymore than the apparatus of literacy is "out there," beyond our control. Both technology and literacy, or technologies of literacy, as the case may be, are produced and reproduced by us, with the broadest sense of agency implied: writing teachers, students, tutors, administrators, technorhetoricians, programmers and software developers, technical support staff and academic computing directors, WAC coordinators, department chairs, curriculum committees, disciplinary faculty, assessment committees, and so on. Christina Haas and Christine Neuwirth (1994) put it well, I think, when they note that "technologies are 'made' through our thinking and talking about them. Consequently they are continually evolving: they are not static but shaped subtly and constantly by the uses to which they are put and by the discourse that accompanies those uses" (p. 324). There really is no such thing as pure, unmediated, application of technology. To apply is to insert oneself into an ideological framework. The question then becomes rather practical and rather difficult: to which framework(s) will writing centers and computers and composition apply?

4

The Idea of an Electronic Writing Center

No living word relates to its object in a *singular* way: between the word and its object, between the word and the speaking subject, there exists an elastic environment of other, alien words about the same object, the same theme. . . . The living utterance, having taken meaning and shape at a particular historical moment in a socially specific environment, cannot fail to brush up against thousands of living dialogic threads, woven by socio-ideological consciousness around the given object of utterance; it cannot fail to become an active participant in social dialogue.

— (Bakhtin, 1981, pp. 276-277)

If, following Bakhtin, we problematize disciplines, if we see disciplines as ongoing projects subject to both the forces of unification and the forces of diversification, we can, I believe, create more productive programs. I believe that it is possible to see writing across the disciplines programs as enhancing learning through encouraging students to connect ideas presented in different disciplines and to connect those ideas with their everyday experiences. . . . It's possible, but given the institutional structure of education and the role it currently plays in our society, it isn't particularly easy.

— (Cooper, 1994, p. 532)

Because the title of this chapter—like the title of the book—bears so much resemblance to Stephen North's 1984 essay, "The Idea of a Writing Center," I feel obliged to make at least one disclaimer before I go on: This chapter will not begin in frustration. In fact, though I admit I've carried my fair share of frustration in this book, particularly as I've contemplated writing center history, the ISA of literacy, the Strategy of Containment, and the Rhetoric of Technocentrism, I have no frustration here, at least not yet, because I will soon be engaging in that rare "scholarly" practice of educational fantasy. So, while North could rail at "members of my profession" who "do not understand what I do" (p. 433), I cannot, in good conscience, accuse anyone for failing to understand what I have not yet done to reformulate the scene of writing. Let me begin, then, with a description of that current scene.

Susan Miller (1991) estimates that approximately five million students take writing courses each year. If each of those students wrote four papers per course, we'd be looking at 20 million papers in composition courses alone (including upper-level and graduate courses). If we included the papers students write in other programs and departments, as writing center directors and WAC directors can't help but do, the number would be even higher. More staggering than the sheer volume, however, is the fate of these papers, which I tend to visualize in stacks, sitting in boxes in hallways or in envelopes taped to office doors—papers that largely go unclaimed at the end of each semester, papers that are easily forgotten by students and T.A.s and professors alike. This is not to suggest that writing papers is a colossal waste of time. But to many students, college writing is just an exercise—a disposable process with little or no consequence outside the course/grade/credit system. The situation is so unremarkable that it hardly seems worth commenting upon.

Writing centers, of course, have done more than just comment upon the relative isolation that is required of this exercise; they have critiqued it by legitimizing the role of collaboration in the composing process. It is a critique that has placed significant pressure on conceptions of learning (Summerfield, 1988); epistemologies of writing (Bruffee, 1984; Lunsford, 1991), the idea of student authorship (Ede, 1989), plagiarism and intellectual independence (Clark, 1988), and other values stemming from traditional, humanism and literary authorship. The legacy of this "subversive" conversation, as Lunsford and Ede described it is, perhaps, the writing center's most under-represented and significant contribution to the teaching of writing.

Nor have writing centers been alone in this endeavor. Computers and composition has also pushed English Studies toward collaborative models of learning and dialogic models of literacy, most often by putting those models into practice. Charlie Moran (1992) points out that until teachers began using computer classrooms, they were stuck with "an impersonal structure" that in no way facilitated collaboration. He calls this structure the brick-and-mortar classroom:

> Facing the classroom teacher-desk, there are student desks, not often, these days, bolted to the floor, but still set in rows. These desks, like the teacher's classroom desk, are 'unreal' work-spaces. They are also poor writing places. The writing surface is often irregular, often small, and, for those who are left-handed, awkwardly placed.

And if one wants to set up small groups, these pieces of furniture suddenly become awAWard and heavy, for they have been built of metal and laminated, wood-grained plastic—to last. (p. 8)

The furniture, the walls, the lack of resources, all this conspires—without truly planning a conspiracy—to make writing and collaborating unnaturally difficult. Barker and Kemp (1990) described the computer classroom, then, as a procedural shift away from the "proscenium" classroom, where students sit in theater-style rows, facing the stage. The physical structure of the room and the configuration of the network also implied a larger pedagogical shift away from lecture or top–down models of learning, toward collaborative or social constructivist models of learning and of discourse. As they point out, the primary activity in a networked writing classroom is not the dissemination of information from the teacher's desk, but intensive text exchange among students.

Yet if writing centers and computers and composition have indeed forged new traditions based on collaborative learning, it is unclear why neither field has yet developed a shared practice that would, in effect, extend the possibilities of collaboration along the lines that Cooper suggests for writing across the disciplines. For example, although some professors, students, and writing programs have begun publishing student essays on the Internet, to my knowledge, no one has considered the fate of these writings in anything but a negative light, as a rebirth of plagiarism, or the term-paper warehouse. No one has re-imagined the fate of those 20 million+ writings in a dialogic sense.

In this chapter, then, I would like to propose that there is a life for student writing beyond the course and the semester; that writing centers and computers and composition could become instruments of this alternative life. The proper use of these writings could affect the ways we approach much of what we do in Composition. Here, I will only be concerned with the impact on the writing center. However, because I am not reporting upon an existing practice, I must confess that the idea of an electronic writing center is, at this point, just an idea for dialogizing the scene of college writing; to begin using the Internet to invite other student voices into our conferences; to create what Andrea Lunsford (1991) calls a "Burkean parlor center" online.

Though I am fairly certain that a proposal such as this has not been made before, I would not say that it is completely without precedent in the writing center literature. Michael Joyner (1991), for example, has already argued for an intertextual approach to tutoring by applying a post-structuralist analysis to social constructivist theory. He says that to offer students membership into a discourse community "is to mislead students into thinking that their texts do not participate in a struggle for power, that we as tutors do not participate in this struggle" (p. 84). In his version of collaboration, "students are informed from the outset that their writing is not a thing to itself" and that "argumentative writing," the "backbone" of academic discourse, is charged with "political dimensions" (p. 87) even when politics are not an explicit theme of the text.

If students are writing essays on parental notification before a minor can obtain an abortion, it is the responsibility of the writing center tutor not simply to read the students' texts and test them against preconceived notions of full development and logical argument, but to inform the students that many texts previously have been generated on this topic and to question them on where they feel their texts enter into this larger arena of discourse and what they contribute to it. Such a locating of texts will offer students a sense of empowerment, a sense that their writing is important and significant. (p. 86)

The point of the conference, Joyner concludes, is not to reach consensus with the dominant, but to situate writing within an "arena of discourse." The intertextual approach to tutoring, then, attempts to empower students by broadening their understanding of how and why they are contributing to a subject in which "many texts have previously been generated." In the very least, Joyner's approach dialogizes the conference by inviting other voices to speak to the student and the tutor.

By contrast, Nancy Welch (1993) has argued that some students who come to the writing center are "already aware, sometimes painfully so, that their meanings are contested" (p. 4). "Even alone," she continues, "these students write with and against a cacophony of voices, collaborating not with another person but with the Otherness of their words" (p. 4). Such students, who are already immersed in an arena of discourse do not need tutors to complicate the scene. Rather, they need what Welch describes as "a space of critical exile" to sort through these demands: "exile means the creation of a space in which we can reflect on and intervene in the languages, conventions, and belief systems that constitute our texts, our sense of self, our notions of what is 'common sense'" (p. 4). Students need a space of critical exile if they are to cut a path through the heteroglossia of voices that surround them.

Though Welch and Joyner may disagree in their approach, they both describe the conference as an interplay of literacies, or a discursive struggle for power that considers Bruffee's (1984) "normal discourse" as one of many discourses to contend with, not the only discourse toward which we students should strive. This is not to say that these models of collaboration reject academic discourse as a matter of principle. As I argued in the previous chapter, all movements toward centripetal discourse can be read, alternately, as movements away from centrifugal discourse. Likewise, as I noted about the practice of email tutoring, the point is not to dismantle centripetal discourse but to disrupt the boundaries of what gets said in the writing conference; to open it up to those centrifugal voicings that students and tutors often suppress. In that light, Joyner and Welch's models for collaboration can be seen as precedents not just for email tutoring but for the electronic writing center, because they both dialogize the writing conference or test the limits of a purely dyadic, interventionist relationship between tutor and student.

It seems to me, however, that larger structural changes are also needed in the ways we collaborate in order to fully realize the agendas Joyner and Welch are advocating. We can create electronic resources to help us pursue dialogic literacy, if and when we decide to do so. Before I get to my analysis of how this might work in individual sessions, I would like to visualize that electronic resource, as it might appear on a writing center homepage.

In my mind's eye, I see a low-tech web site with a brief welcome message, a search engine, and a list of broad subject-areas to browse through: AIDS, African-American Studies, architecture, behaviorism, Christianity, The Civil War, ethics in the professions, gender, racism, Renaissance, science and society, technology, etc. If this *could* be construed as a web site for writing across the curriculum, several factors nevertheless make that conclusion a bit hasty: the writings collected here are not categorized by discipline but by subject, there is no advice or policies on writing instruction or assessment, and there are writings from more than one university. In short, what we have is a simple, bare-bones, collection of undergraduate student writings. If it is not a peer-reviewed anthology, an e-journal, an official writing program site, a resource page for teachers and students, on OWL, a class web site, or a personal homepage, then what is it? And how could it work in the writing center?

THE INTERTEXTUAL APPROACH

In order to illustrate one way to use an EWC in a writing conference, let me begin by restating the dilemma I faced when I tried to tutor Anne. Then I will reframe that dilemma by triangulating our conversation with other student texts. In the process, I hope to situate our conversation in that larger arena of discourse that Joyner described peviously.

In my analysis of that session, readers may recall that most of the exchange was focused not on dialogic connections but on academic angst: defending claims, flushing out contradictions, providing detailed evidence, and so on. Lurking beneath these apparently generic concerns about academic writing, however, were more specific concerns about the making of knowledge in literary criticism, or Anne's role as literary critic in English Studies. Take the following passage as an example.

> Most notable among the plays "Winter's Night," Desire Under The Elms, Long Day's Journey Into Night, and The Little Foxes, was the explicit gender roles existing between men and women. The women were the keepers of the house, the men were keepers of the family. These differing roles had a major impact on the family structure. Women are depicted as dependent on men for stability and financial security. The woman is supposed to be grateful that she is being taken care of. She is supposed to be attentive to the needs of her husband and should happily fulfill those needs. Any assertion of individual identity or ownership is dismissed. For example, Eugene O'neill's character, Abbie is primarily concerned with having a "home." Being married is her ticket to living well.

There are very few references to O'Neill or any other playwright in this passage, beyond the perfunctory identification of Abbie as his character. The absence of references to the author, however, is problematic, not just because it impedes Anne's understanding of intention and genre, but because it limits her maneuverability within the subject of gender and family life. In one of my posts to Anne, I asked "why do the authors create these portraits of the American family? (you already discussed 'how'....maybe now it's time to start thinking of why they did it?)" It is a question she really cannot answer very well, even as an English major. Toward the end of the essay, we might recall, she simply equates these portrayals of women in the theater with reality. When pressed, she later pulls back from that position, perhaps recognizing her mistake: "As far as the overall tone to the paper, my main point (hopefully) was that women were constrained within that time period. And I don't think that women in life accepted the roles handed to them. Women as portrayed within literature did."

It could be argued, then, that what Anne needs—what anyone struggling with disciplinary discourse needs—is sound advice on how to work with the conventions. But again, I want to challenge the assumption that the only way to establish power in writing is to appropriate a centripetal, disciplinary discourse. I won't deny the validity or even the utility of such discourses: Indeed, I spent many weeks on email helping Anne understand the conventions of literary criticism and political science. Yet, in many ways, I now believe that our work in that area may have actually impeded Anne's overall ideological growth as a writer. In fact, I'll go so far as to say that what Anne needed was not rhetorical advice on the genre but some sense, as Joyner might say, that her writing was not a thing in itself but in fact participated in a larger arena of discourse. Though it is possible, using Joyner's method, to simply represent this larger arena to the student through a discussion of other (professional) writers' work, as they are filtered through the tutor, I believe there is another way to bring that arena of discourse into the conference.

What would have happened, for example, if instead of talking more about critical strategies, we could have linked to the EWC site and clicked on the subject heading, "Gender"? Then, having navigated through the choices, we came upon an essay by Kevin Nguyen, which was written in Nick Evans literature class at the University of Texas-Austin. How might Kevin's discussion of Charlotte Perkins Gilmans' novel, *The Yellow Wallpaper* have affected our tutorial conversation about drama? In what ways do these excerpts from Kevin's paper both support and contradict Anne's claims that women of the 19th century were constrained by patriarchy?

GILMAN: A NEW PERSPECTIVE ON EMERSONIAN IDEAS

The great writer Ralph Waldo Emerson once wrote, "trust thyself: every heart vibrates to that iron string" (p. 1033). How surprised he would be to find out that a half century later this type of idea would culminate in a growing restlessness among American women unsatisfied with their lives and with their roles in society - a society dominated by men with little or no place for women outside the home. One of these female writers who helped lead the battle for domestic and social reform was Charlotte Perkins Gilman. One of her more particularly forceful works is "The Yellow Wall-Paper," meant to highlight the submissive and highly undervalued role women play in marriages at the time. Through this work, Gilman expressed her inner frustrations with the servitude women had to endure in their marriages during that time period, and she advocated her own brand of Emersonian non-conformity for women. By taking such a profoundly dismal outlook on married life, Gilman hoped to inspire other women to seek new roles not only in the domestic, but also public, arena. "The Yellow Wall-Paper" represents to a large degree what the feminist movement of the late 19th century was about, and by analyzing both the story and context of its creation, it becomes apparent the type of interpretation Gilman made of Emerson's work "Self-Reliance."

Although "The Yellow Wall-Paper" focuses on a wife's sudden decline into madness, the story brings forth a very important issue - that of women's roles not only in domestic life, but in society as well. It becomes abundantly apparent even from the first few lines of the story that the wife's views concern her place in the marriage when she says "John laughs at me" for worrying about the house (p. 801). In fact, he laughs at her several times throughout the story whenever she expresses concern or worry. This further indicates the dominant role he holds in the marriage. Her opinions are further subjugated by the fact that her husband is a physician, and "practical in the extreme" (p. 801). Therefore, the narrator feels as if she is doubly inferior, both as a wife and as a patient, and that she must take her husband's advice no matter how strong her own concerns. In fact, even her mental activities such as writing are regulated because her husband "hates to have [her] write a word" (p. 802). Even in her own family she can find no solace because her brother, also a physician, sides with her husband. . . .

All of these symbolic and hidden meanings transform a simple story into a banner decrying the necessity of sociological reform in attitudes and treatment of women at the turn of the century. Charlotte Perkins Gilman helped paved the way for equality towards women with this and numerous other works. Particularly, Gilman used this story as a vehicle to denounce "women's economic dependence inside marriage, their unpaid and therefore undervalued work in the home" (p. 799).

But what caused her and many other daughters of post-Civil War America to suddenly seek a new meaning in life? During the Civil War, these docile homemakers often followed their men into service and acted as nurses, cooks, and clothes washers in the armies. The ones that stayed at home tended the crops or helped secure supplies for the armies. After the Civil War, women found "increased educational and employment opportunities available to them" and increased "involvement in political and reform activities" (p. 15). This taste of freedom from the shackles of a domestic life inspired women who "increasingly moved outside the home to claim a place in the public world" (p. 15). These women, inspired by the writings of authors such as Gilman and Alcott, came seeking equality. They fought for these reforms through political, social, and literary means. These reforms were helped in part by a new style of writing called "realism" developed in the later half of the 19th century. This style of writing responded to "the sweeping economic, social, and political changes of post - war life" (p. 11). This new era in literature opened up the door for many reform movements and finally allowed women a forum to express their views to America. Therefore, Charlotte Perkins Gilman was a voice of her times.

In addition, Gilman sought to use aspects of her own personal life to inspire women to seek change. For example, her narrator's respectful/frustrated attitude towards her hysician husband evokes the type of encounters she had with doctors in her own life.

When Gilman experienced severe depression in her marriage, her doctor recommended that she "devote herself to domestic work...and 'never touch pen, brush, or pencil as long as you live'" which nearly "drove her...to the brink of 'utter mental ruin'" (p. 799). From the viewpoint of this contextual background, it becomes clear that "The Yellow Wall-Paper" is not only "a subtle analysis of the power politics of marriage" but also "an indictment of the medical treatment she received and...medical attitudes towards women" (p. 799). These types of messages follow the ideas espoused by Emerson a half-century earlier in his "Self-Reliance." Charlotte Gilman could even be described as a social offspring of the ideas and goals brought forth by Emerson. Gilman sought social, political, and especially ideological changes in attitudes towards women. It was Emerson who said "consistency is the hobgoblin of little minds" and that belief in oneself is "the essence of genius, of virtue, and of life" (p. 1037, 1039). Obviously Gilman wanted to help women achieve such genius by inspiring them to change their lives and public attitudes, allowing them the freedom to choose who they want to be.

Perhaps, the most obvious thing to say about this paper, in relation to our tutorial, is that it supports Anne's central thesis that women were constrained by their time period. Clearly, Gilman's character suffers a malady that is not so much biological as it is sociological. Especially interesting, in this regard, is the husband's notion that the wife should refrain from writing while in the house, a detail that we later learn was taken from Gilman's own life. The straightforward application of this paper, then, would be to employ it as a form of support, so that Anne could make her case about patriarchy even stronger, perhaps along these lines: What was happening in drama was also happening in the novel. Therefore, it must be true.

In another light, though, Kevin's paper does not really amplify Anne's argument but contradicts it, which is, I think, more interesting. In the first paragraph, for example, he notes that Gilman was "one of these female writers who helped lead the battle for domestic and social reform." What, by contrast, did O'Neill do? Why did he write? Likewise, in Kevin's conclusion he notes that other "women, inspired by the writings of authors such as Gilman and Alcott, came seeking equality." When he says that Gilman's was a "voice of the times," then, he lends credence to his earlier assertion that there was, indeed, a feminist movement in the 19th century that took issue with patriarchy. Anne's conclusion about the same time period, however, is much different:

Literature can be a reflection of the society and the time. Women were constrained in the period between 1865 and 1900. Women weren't allowed to vote, if they didn't marry who would take care of them? The idea that a man should provide for his wife is ingrained. Women were offered no alternative.

Unlike Kevin, Anne foregrounds the stability, rather than the instability, of gender roles in the family and in literature. The point of this comparison is not to determine who is right—Kevin or Anne, Gilman or O'Neill. Obviously, there is room for complexity when the subject is gender. The point is that this paper could have helped Anne and I engage the subject of gender differently, to dialogize what appears to be a straightforward conclusion based upon her work in a single class. Essentially, this activity brings together two students of English, one in New York, the other in Texas, through the idea of an electronic writing center.

In more symbolic ways, the activity also brings together two courses, two professors, and two departments of English. Though it does all this in a fairly typical way, through the reading of ɩ n essay produced some time prior to my conversation with Anne, there is no reason to rule out more direct contact with student writers; no reason to assume that Kevin would not want to respond to an email message from Anne or me. Others have already described interclass partnerships between students in different geographical locations. But to my knowledge, no one has studied or even suggested intertutorial partnerships, or informal electronic links between writing centers that are established, sustained, and terminated by the tutors and students who do the work.

What seems especially exciting about the idea of these partnerships is not just the bridging of geographical distances but the bridging of disciplinary distances. If, as Marilyn Sternglass (1997) suggests in her longitudinal study of CUNY students, a writer can make knowledge by applying what she learned in one discipline to another disciplinary context, then why limit Anne's prospects to the discipline of English? If the point is to bring other voices into the tutorial, why stop with one voice? What would have happened, then, if we had returned to the EWC page and selected another paper? Take, for example, Julie A. Johnson's essay, published in the undergraduate, interdisciplinary journal, *CoyotE*, at the University of South Dakota. How would the excerpts from this history paper complicate our conversation about gender roles? How would Julie's presentation of history, including her reading of some primary sources, dialogize Anne's presentation of literature?

WOMEN AND THE CONFEDERACY

It is not known how many women actually participated in battle; however, the number seems to be higher than anyone expected. These women played the role of the warrior and literally gave up their gender to fight. One such case is Amy Clark. She dressed like a man to serve in the Confederate army with her husband. After his death, she continued her service and was wounded and captured by the Union. Once the North discovered her true identity, they released her back into the Southern army and insisted that she wear a dress. Some say that Amy Clark may have worn lieutenant's bars on her uniform. Another women who dressed as a man to fight was Malenda Blalock, who posed as a brother to her husband. Another southern female warrior was

Madame Loreta Janeta Velazquez, also known as Lieutenant Henry Buford. She raised her own cavalry and fought in the Battle of Bull Run. After being wounded twice, she joined in on another activity in which an elite group of southern women participated: espionage. . . .

As women struggled with the roles they had to assume during the war, they thought about other roles as well, such as love and marriage. A nineteen-year-old girl wrote in her diary that she would rather be an old maid and prove to the world that life can be wonderful without a man taking care of a woman. Women make fools of themselves for their men so without the men, women would act less foolish. Sarah Morgan saw her own "shocking ignorance and pitiful inferiority" and became upset because she was not given the same opportunities as men, especially in education. However, even though women suffered from feelings of inferiority, they knew how important it was for them to stand by their men, especially during times of war. . . .

Southern women are not given enough recognition for what they had accomplished during the Civil War. They seem to get much more attention for supposedly prostituting themselves than for actually fighting in battles or for nursing the Confederate soldiers back to health. The myth of the South is that women were like those from Gone With the Wind, but they were not in dress and attitude. However, most Southern women did possess the passion, the drive, and the desire to commit themselves to the Confederacy and supported their loved ones any way they knew how.

More so than the Kevin's essay on Gilman, this essay on the Civil War opens an interesting fissure between literature and reality, fiction and history. Julie's main point is that the Civil War created new opportunities for women to be something other than wives and mothers. In many ways, it picks up where my session with Anne left off, at that intersection between fiction and truth, or representation and reality. Consider, for example, the question I posed to Anne late in the transcript:

ahh, see this is very interesting to me —the way you phrase it. "I don't think that women in life accepted the roles handed to them. Women in literature did." This raises intriguing questions to me about who these authors were, and how their view of the family fits in with (or somehow misrepresents) what real women did. You suggest that things were different in real life: I tend to agree. But how might we prove this? Are there any testimonials from the time? perhaps revisionary histories of the 19th century?

This question, you might recall, did not lead us into a dialogic framework for interaction. It did not spur on the conversation or make us answerable to each other. Had we been able to triangulate the discussion through Julie's paper, though, this question might have actually become a substantial thread.

Of course, I can only speculate how such a thread could have helped Anne write her paper, but since this is my educational fantasy, I don't see why I shouldn't speculate. Ideally, this conversational thread would have intrigued her? Just as likely, it could have lionized her to re-assert her more limited objectives: "Ok, Dave, you win. Women weren't so constrained in reality. Maybe they did fight in the Civil War. But I'm only concerned with the way women were portrayed in drama. So back off!" This is, of course, an entirely reasonable response, with or without the perturbed inflection. After all, undergraduates have not been authorized to think outside the immediate goal of meeting the criteria of their assignments. In a world of either/or, the choice is simple: either you meet the criteria or you blow it off. My invitation to consider historical evidence, then, could easily be seen by Anne as an invitation to ignore her assignment. But this isn't an either/or decision.

ELECTRONIC EXILE

In my earlier discussion of email "tutoring," I argued that the method works when it creates opportunities for students and tutors to pursue internally persuasive discourse. Dialogic literacy, or the Rhetoric of Answerability, as I conceived it in Chapter Two, was not about changing what students wrote in their final papers, but about changing the parameters of what got said—or, in the case of email tutoring, written—during the conference. Small acts of resistance, in my view, were significant, even within the context of finishing an assignment because they allowed students to resituate themselves in relation to their subjects. That is, email "tutoring" encouraged a creative fissure between the self who wrote the paper and the self who wrote the email messages, allowing the student and, in some cases, the tutor, to explore alternative subject-positions in writing. Through these readings of other student writings, I believe we could have achieved similar results with Anne.

If the intertextual approach to the EWC attempts to connect students to something larger than themselves, or to complicate the ways in which they relate to their subjects, by showing them alternative ways of writing about the subject, the "electronic exile" approach, based on Welch's idea of "critical exile" does the opposite. It works when students (and tutors) have already established a rich interplay of competing voices and need to sort through the different sounds they hear. Bakhtin's conception of language is instructive, in this regard: "For any individual consciousness," he says, "language is not an abstract system of normative forms but rather a concrete heteroglot conception of the world. All words have the 'taste' of a profession, a genre, a tendency, a party, a particular work, a particular person, a generation, an age group, the day and hour" (p. 293). His emphasis on appropriation is equally instructive, especially as we reconsider the session with Katie: To Bakhtin, "the word in language is half someone else's. It becomes 'one's own' only when the speaker populates it with his own intention, his own accent, when he appropriates the word, adapting it to his own semantic and expressive intention" (p. 293). What Katie and I struggled to resolve in that particular session, then, were the "tastes" we both have for the professions of English, Africana Studies, Education and the personal "tendencies" we have for creative writing and academic writing. Ultimately, we struggled to appropriate the discourses on poetics, pedagogy, and race against the conceptual horizons of each other.

Katie's main concern, you may recall, was to develop a teaching guide on discrimination for students grades 6–12. However, as she also made clear, "There is not one right or perfect age at which to begin discussing discrimination," a point I will return to later. Here, I just want to emphasize Katie's interest in the larger context of discrimination. Further evidence comes from her text, specifically, her use of personal information (the story about teaching her daughter about AIDS), her insistence in applying Black poetry to other contexts where discrimination exists, and her interest in relating the concept of disability to discrimination (in part, because her own status as a learning-disabled student, and also because of her experience in another course on computing and disability). These and other statements suggest a need to integrate personal experience into an academic framework, specifically, her experience as a mother, a poet, and a learning-disabled student. Moreover, they illustrate what Bakhtin means when he says "language has been shot through with intentions and accents" (p. 293). To write this teaching guide, Katie must write through, with, or around these competing intentions and accents.

Her feeling of being overwhelmed by these accents, which she makes clear in her opening post, also suggests that Katie is writing in a contested space, as Welch says of her students, amidst a cacophony of voices. Katie's reference to her draft as an "unmanageable document" and her reference to herself as "TRYING TO ACCOMPLISH TOO MUCH" encouraged me, as well, to perceive the cacophony of voices as forces to subdue. I could afford to take this position, I felt, because I perceived the rhetorical task more narrowly than Katie, and, in some ways, more antagonistically, as one of persuading reluctant public school teachers to "do something" about discrimination during Black History Month. Because Katie also intimated that this draft was headed toward publication in an academic journal, I became keenly aware of the non-academic sound to Katie's draft. Here is a sample of what I based my reaction upon:

> We all need to be ourselves first. Therein lies the magic blueprint for creating a place within where justice can dwell, from which we can clean house, ridding our hearts of the fears, misconceptions, and misunderstandings that separate us from our brothers and sisters. The Christian Church (as well as other faiths) offers that opportunity, but Christ's teachings are not appropriate in public schools. There has to be a secular way for educators to exorcise the disease of prejudice and liberate truth from the souls we teach. One such way, is to teach the history of the Civil Rights Movement. . . . Public school teachers, whether working in Alaska, the South Bronx, or Yeehaw Junction, Florida need to incorporate dialogue on prejudice and discrimination throughout grade levels and throughout the school year; such topics should not just be hauled out, dusted off, and paid attention to during February, Black History Month. IF WE DO NOT STUDY HISTORY, WE ARE DOOMED TO REPEAT IT.

In these passages, Katie attaches herself to those larger Civil Rights projects of the 1960s, in my view, by using a rhetoric of Christian conversion—"to exorcise the disease of prejudice and liberate the truth from the souls we teach"—and a rhetoric of moral emergency—"IF WE DO NOT STUDY HISTORY, WE ARE DOOMED TO REPEAT IT." My reaction to these devices, however, was negative:

> What I'm getting at is this: if you want to convince other people to take up this unit I think you need to be more brief, more explicit, and less dramatic. For example, the paragraphs that began with "the single most important thing we can do for humanity" began to feel like a cliché. I'm sure that within the context of teaching, students might agree with your solution —to listen more, share, etc. But as an academic argument, I think you need more.

Of course, if Katie's task could be narrowly conceived in the way I imagined, and only in that way, then perhaps I could stick by my advice. However, as it turns out, her audience in this independent study project was not really a group of teachers but herself and her professor, as we learned at the conclusion of the session. Perhaps that explains her defense of the safe classroom, or more broadly, her interest in using the email session to affirm her ideas about teaching black poetry in a safe classroom, rather than using the session to put those ideas to the test of critical (academic) scrutiny. When I challenged Katie's use of black poetry, her understanding of poetics, and her construction of the classroom, that is, I challenged her very purpose in writing. If, as I argued in Chapter Two, this nevertheless produced an interesting tension in our dialogue—what I called a Rhetoric of Answerability—it also seems reasonable to wonder what this Rhetoric failed to produce. Or, to put it another way, at what price do Katie and I connect dialogically? Are there other ways in which we could have connected?

What would have happened, for example, if we had accessed Rhonda William's paper, which appeared in the online publication, *Intertext*, at Syracuse University. How would this story of a school board meeting, in which race was at issue, have influenced our conversation? Conversely, how might our conversation and Katie's teaching guide have affected Rhonda's writing?

NO MARCH ON WASHINGTON

It was my junior year of high school. Three-hundred-sixty-five days before I graduated leaving behind those same tired faces, away from the monotonous routine of going from locker, to homeroom, to class, to class, to locker, to home. When did I go home anyway? After all the tutorials, extra-curricular activities, and sports, I don't remember spending very much time there. Well, you get the point, high school had really worn me out. Eighth grade is way too early to start high school. By the time you've reached the eleventh grade, you've already developed the impatience of a senior.

My junior year of high school started off rather peacefully. Everyone went about their own routines, hypnotized by the sound of the bell which programmed our daily lives. Lunch was even good (that is, good rated on lunchroom standards), meat actually looked like meat, and the old ladies that served us were actually nice (that is, we hadn't made them bitter yet).

Homework for the night? Get Teacher/Student/Parent Contracts signed, and fill out insurance forms. Wow, what a heavy load. Friends stuck close to old time cliques, or to new ones which started over the summer, and summer love still lingered in the air.

We didn't know, however, that turbulence was surrounding us. Those who were lucky found out early; they had inside connections, such as PTO parents or fanatical community leaders. Others read articles in our local paper that suggested community unrest: "ANGRY PARENTS FIGHT BACK!" The people who knew nothing found out when they drove past orange ribbons that hung from trees, or when they were attacked by reporters at the end of the day. Dwight Morrow High School's fate was suddenly placed in the hands of its students, the judges, and neighboring communities. Everyone had a viewpoint, and all wanted their voice to be heard.

"Board Meeting Tonight, Members of the Board and the Englewood Community Discuss Regionalization", read fliers on the school's walls. "Please students, don't forget to tell your parents to come and support our students, our schools, and our community," the principal pleaded over the loud speaker at the end of the day.

For the first time in approximately ten years the issue of regionalization between Englewood's school system and neighboring Tenafly was rekindled. Was it finally time for the 97% minority Dwight Morrow High School, and the predominantly white Tenafly High, to join forces as one to learn, walk, and teach together? If so, students of many ages would be forced to bus to new schools with new faces forced to learn about cultures outside of their own. Many would argue that meeting new people and sharing differences is enriching, that it broadens your horizons. But, what happens when differences are viewed through the eyes of racists? Who wants to sit on a bus, share the same bathrooms, texts, and teachers with people who believe that the word "nigger" means Black, and should be capitalized to represent a nationality? This was the fear of many Englewood parents, because the majority of Tenafly had a history of not liking or accepting African Americans. (If you're assuming that this story took place in the 1960s, I've painted a clear picture).

Tenafly parents were enraged with the idea of sending their kids to Englewood schools. I'm sure that they had many issues of concern--issues that come with being a parent. The most obvious issue, however, was race. "ENGLEWOOD STUDENTS CAN'T LEARN," was the outcome of most of Tenafly's private meetings. We were very rarely informed or invited to their meetings; however, we often left our meeting doors open for them. So you can imagine, what a kick-in-the-ass reading this type article must have been. "What do they mean we can't learn?" many of us asked. "Since when did Dwight Morrow become a school for the mentally disabled??" At times, statements like this, did nothing but empower us to do better. Sometimes, we'd get burnt out from having to always prove ourselves. A student can never learn the true meaning of the words teachers, and principals constantly utter, "Be on your best behavior, you're representing our school," until you've been through a situation like this one. A situation made up of pins and needles.

It was a confusing time for most of us. I remember sitting down one day, and conversing with a white girl from Tenafly I had met during the track season. "Guess what," she says after a moment's conversation, "A few weeks ago a freshman girl got caught with acid in her locker. I was shocked. I couldn't believe that stuff like that happened at those schools. I never recalled anyone from my school, since I've been there, getting involved in something that deep. Anyway, it was a confusing time, especially for the large number of intelligent, well behaved students. We often found ourselves not knowing when to stand tall, or bow our heads in shame. Many of us found ourselves voicing out at public meetings about the rewards of Dwight Morrow High School, but when asked during private hours what school we attended, we would lower our voices and simply reply "Englewood." We were afraid of the images they had or would conjure up. It was at both the moments of pride and the moments of shame that I realized that my days at Dwight Morrow were in counting. Suddenly the faces didn't seem so old and tired, and I began to enjoy the monotony of going to my locker. I even found myself associating with people I never associated with before. I could tell by the looks on everyones faces that I wasn't drifting in this boat alone.

I went to the meeting that night. My parents did too. Our auditorium was filled to its capacity. I made my way through the cameras and reporters and took a seat in the back. Surrounding me were fellow members of my community, opposite me were strangers covered in orange and white (Tenafly's colors), from the shoes on their feet to the paint on their faces. Most of them held signs which read "ENGLEWOOD STUDENT'S CAN'T LEARN," "WE WILL ONLY ACCEPT THE BEST," "ENGLEWOOD'S BOARD MEMBERS ARE MONKEYS," and things of that nature. (If you're waiting for me to tell you about the civil rights speech Martin Luther King Junior gave at Dwight Morrow High School that night, I waited just as patiently too.? The animosity in the room was as thick as the fog outside. I remember observing a scene where one of the African American members of my community sat peacefully in his chair, and a Caucasian woman from Tenafly stood over him, hanging her sign directly above his head. The peaceful Englewood member asked the Tenafly member to kindly remove the sign from over his head. After asking more than twice, it was obvious that the Tenafly member was purposely being rude. Like dynamite ready to explode, the man slowly rose out of his chair and turned around. He snatched the sign out of her hand, ripped it to pieces, and proceeded to do a dance of some sort on top of them, and left. The Englewood crowd began to cheer and roar. I don't believe that he handled the matter in the most mature way, but she received the treatment she asked for. The lady stood there, stupidly, and in silence.

"Englewood students are ignorant, incompetent fools and I will not have my child go to school with them!" a loud mouth Tenafly lady hollered. Englewood made many remarks too, but none of that sort. They were intelligent, well thought out responses, and it was obvious who the ignorant ones were. As I scanned the orange faces in the room, I noticed that there were no Tenafly students to be found. I recalled the girl who sat Indian-style with me on the lawn at the track meet, and innocently told me the story of the freshman from her school that was caught with acid. Why wasn't she there? A stern black woman stood from her chair. Her dreadlocks hung down her back, and swayed with the rhythm of her words, and the motion of her head. She pointed distinctively toward the Tenafly crowd. "I can't make the judge's decision for him, but I'm sure he would understand that I can not send my child to a school where she is going to be oppressed every day of her life. I don't know what kind of an example you think you're setting for your kids, Tenafly, but I will not stand here and let you persecute these innocent kids because of your ignorance. Englewood kids are intelligent, kind, and can compete with your kids any day."

A sense of pride came me over me. The Englewood crowd clapped and rose to their feet. A shrill voice called out, "Sit down lady!"

"Yeah, and shut up!" another one chimed in. (If you've already pictured members of the Ku Klux Clan racing down the aisles of my auditorium on their horses, fire in hand, then I need not give you anymore depiction, and you probably know just how I felt.)

The whole ordeal is over now, and I probably can't give you any statistics about Englewood's or Tenafly's school system budget cuts, test scores, things of that sort. I left the meeting that night with those images and sounds of hate running through my head, and felt the blow from them in my heart. I stood outside and waited for my parents to pull the car around. It was very difficult to see the color of the cars. Everyone was squinting their eyes and pushing, trying to see if it was their car that pulled up beside them. Though anger besieged our hearts, I noticed that everyone stood side by side in front of "Martin Luther King Hall Auditorium," and I thought, "Wouldn't it be nice, if God placed a sheet of fog over the eyes of people who took for granted the beauty and importance of color."

Many weeks, and thousands of dollars later, the courts ruled against regionalization of Englewood's school system. Everything we did, now seems futile. Englewood and Tenafly wasted so much money on legal fees fighting for the separation and integration of our school systems, and it seems as though it would've been more beneficial financially, socially, and most important mentally, to have spent the thousands of dollars on the students already enrolled in their schools. All we have to show for the time and money spent are two quiet communities, separated by a dim fire waiting to be rekindled.

I left the meeting that night; I didn't get to hear Martin Luther King Junior's civil rights speech. He had been dead for almost thirty years, but I knew in my heart that where he was, he was preaching. I also didn't get to sit next to any brave heroes like Rosa Parks, but my mind still sees the images of those orange faces, and my ears still ring of racial slurs. I didn't march down the streets that night either chanting no Old Negro Spirituals, or even raise my voice in protest, but I sure could feel my kinfolk calling.

Earlier, I promised that I would return to Katie's point that there is no right age to begin a discussion of discrimination. I believe Rhonda's portrayal of the Tenafly parents, in this story, amply demonstrates that point. As well, Rhonda's paper seems to provide testimonial evidence for Katie's other generalizations. Rhonda's use of historical references, for example, lends credence to Katie's rhetoric of moral emergency—"If we don't study history we are doomed to repeat it." Clearly, Rhonda feels that history is repeating itself at this school board meeting. And Rhonda's invocation of Civil Rights heroes getting ready to preach and KKK members getting ready to form a posse also validates Katie's rhetoric of conversion—"to exorcise the disease of prejudice." Overall, the paper paints a vivid picture of the ways in which racism perpetuates itself in a public school. Though Rhonda's essay is not about teaching or Black poetry, it is about Black people and their extensive history with discrimination. In fact, one could even argue that Rhonda's story about "regionalization" is exactly the kind of story that Katie wants to prevent from reoccurring, through her own efforts to teach students about discrimination.

If indeed this is the case that Rhonda's essay confirms Katie's assumptions, would it not also contradict the direction of our tutorial conversation? Wouldn't our debate over pedagogy and poetics seem a bit overkill or petty when, as Rhonda demonstrates, real lives are being disrupted because of the ignorance that Katie warns against? If, in other words, my dialogic interaction with Katie was based on my skeptical reading of her intentions, wouldn't Rhonda's paper kill that skepticism?

There are no sure things when it comes to educational fantasy. But I am inclined to see Rhonda's paper, and the "real life" context that it represents, as a provocative challenge to the dialogic literacy of the session. I would not want to choose, or make Katie choose, between me or Rhonda—clearly, the interplay of all three of us would be most interesting. What I am suggesting, finally, is that an EWC could be a site of critical exile not just for writers but for writers and tutors who are stuck in their own conversational rhythms. It is true, I would argue, that a Rhetoric of Answerability can dialogize the conference and encourage students and tutors to produce internally persuasive discourses. But it also seems true that there is only so much we can see on each other's conceptual horizons. Dialogic literacy can become a limiting frame, especially when the tutor and student have different conceptions of the rhetorical task—different "tastes" of discourse in their mouths, as Bakhtin might say.

This tension is heightened, or antagonized, depending on your point of view, by the demands of academic writing, as my reaction to Katie's off-stage voices suggests. But as Alice Gillam (1991) has shown, in "Writing Center Ecology: A Bakhtinian Perspective," such hazards can be reconceived generatively. In the session Gillam analyzes, the student writer is composing an essay on the ways she reads the Bible. The tutor, "herself an aspiring fiction writer, feels pulled between [the student's] mesmerizing narrative voice and the teacher's expectation for focus and unity of theme" (p. 5). As a fiction writer, she wants to encourage Mary's narrative voice. But as a tutor she wants Mary to succeed academically. Mary, herself, wants to succeed academically, so the tutor, Belinda, "feels she has no choice but to encourage Mary to 'normalize' her voice so that it can be heard and found acceptable in the academy" (p. 5). But Gillam critiques this solution, arguing that "the richness of voice and detail may hold the key to focus. Rather than stripping her 'story' to the bone in order to impose focus, perhaps Mary needs to flesh out the contradictions embedded in the text and puzzle over the off-key shifts in voice as a way of discovering focus. A Bakhtinian perspective," she concludes, "might have allowed Belinda to help Mary see the dissonances in voice and narrative as opportunities to dialogize and clarify meaning rather than as the enemies of focus, as forces to be subdued and 'normalized'" (p. 7). The key to focus, in other words, lies not in denying those centrifugal voicings but in celebrating them.

It could be argued, of course, that one does not need an EWC to do what Gillam suggests. If the point is to offer the student a critically reflexive space to sort through those different voices, then one does not need to look at other students' papers. But if the point is triangulate the tutorial conversation, or to interrupt the privacy of that exchange, then I dare say we need to build electronic spaces that can become windows to the world outside the writing center. Of course, one can achieve this by simply lining a bookshelf or visiting the library, but I think that misses the point. A writing center is a writing center because it is not another traditional academic forum; because it foregrounds student concerns and provides students with an alternative to grades, competition, and the authority of teachers and books. Is there any reason to think that this alternative scene of learning should exclude the voices of students who came before?

ANOTHER REASON TO COME TO THE WRITING CENTER

I have argued, so far, that student writings can play a valuable role in the conference. But what about the writers who do not need conferences? What about Rhonda, for example? Could she have been motivated to write a different conclusion in her paper, had she known that a white parent at SUNY-Albany was not just training to be a teacher but was also preparing to fight the kind of ignorance that was evident at the school board meeting? Even if Rhonda took less of a shine to Katie's ideas, how could they have helped each other in ways that no tutor, working as a tutor, could have done? What do we gain by keeping such students apart? If we want an electronic space that does more than contain writing problems—that is, if we want to bring writers into the center who do not necessarily need "tutoring" but who nevertheless need a dialogic exchange, what can we do?

The sessions that I discussed previously, as I mentioned earlier, were all conducted at SUNY-Albany between 1992 and 1995. To answer that last question, though, I want to tell a story about where I currently work, at the Illinois Institute of Technology. Like many technical schools, IIT is dominated by men, both in the student body and in the faculty—men from all over the world, with sizable populations from America, of course, but also from Europe, India and Pakistan, the Middle East, South Korea, and so on. The story I want tell, then, is the story of a woman who took my class, "The Self in Language." This course features readings by psychologists, poets, linguists, rhetoricians, and other writers, who all focus on the construction of self in oral and written language. It is a course designed for students to meet general education requirements in the Department of Humanities.

During the semester that Dana took the course, I had assigned a chapter from the book *Women's Ways of Knowing*, by Mary Field Belenky, Blythe McVicker Clinchy, Nancy Rule Goldberger, and Jill Mattuck Tarule (1986). When it came time for students to produce their final papers, Dana decided to work with this book by imitating the authors' methodologies and testing their claims. She did so by interviewing a dozen women—students, mothers, professionals, some combination—asking each one how they construed themselves *as selves*, in relation to gender and language. The mothers spoke mostly about their families and their connections with their children or husbands, and the professionals spoke mostly about getting ahead in the workplace, despite gender discrimination. With the exception of the students, then, the women construed themselves differently depending on whether they were talking about the home or the workplace, thus contradicting Belenky et. al.'s claim that women naturally tend toward "connected knowing." The career-oriented women that Dana interviewed clearly saw themselves as independent, autonomous selves, sharing more in common with the (essentialist) masculinity than the (essentialist) femininity.

In this context, I am not interested in discussing Dana's claims or the limits of liberal feminism. I have already illustrated with my discussion of the other sessions the ways in which other writings could be used to dialogize the conference. Here, I want to focus on Dana's position as a writer and as a woman at IIT. Her decision to interview other women, for example, suggests an interest in squaring her experience in the class with her experience outside the class, applying these theories of the self to the lives of real people. What would have happened, though, if Dana had an electronic writing center to work with as she wrote her final paper? How might she have construed her task differently if she could have juxtaposed her findings with those generated by another student-researcher at another school?

Earlier, in my discussion of the intertextual approach, I argued that an EWC could broaden the context in which students write, making visible what teachers have always taken for granted: a larger arena of discourse. In the context of IIT, where the ratio of women to men is rather small, and it is not unusual for a teacher to have only two or three women in a seminar of 15, there is another layer to consider. An EWC could not only connect these women to a larger arena of discourse but to a larger network of women writers. In this way, an EWC could break down gender barriers that are sustained by our institution and the professions it serves. The signal this sends to other concerned faculty is that there are other reasons to send writers to the center.

I have time for a brief illustration of the point. Imagine that during the course of writing her paper, Dana had read Jean Forrest's paper, also published in the student journal, *Intertext*. In this paper, Jean says that the homemakers in Japan, unlike career-oriented women, have much more autonomy in their lives and much more sense of purpose: "It is when a woman is finally married that she has control over her life." To Jean however, this says more about cultural biases in Japan than it says about the psychological development of self. Or rather, to talk about concepts like autonomy or connection, one needs to talk about the self-in-relation to culture. Describing her own experience working at a hotel in Japan with "office ladies" or OLs, as they are referred to, Jean explains how the women think about themselves as selves, in much the same way that Dana described the American women's feelings, through an interview. Her results, however, say more about the differences between Japan and America, then they say about the differences between Dana and Jean.

THE OFFICE LADY IN JAPAN

After about a year in my position, I spent time with each one of my female staff to do an evaluation. At the end of the evaluation, I asked each of them their career goals, in the short-term and in the long-term. None of them showed any enthusiasm to move ahead, or to be in a position of more power and responsibility. Not one could foresee leaving the current position that they were in, and had no desire to leave. They wanted to do their job, improve if possible, and be comfortable until the time they got married or had a child, at which time they would be retiring from their career. At first this was really difficult for me to understand, but as time passes and you feel the pressure of your peers around you, you soon understand that life would be very uncomfortable living outside of the acceptable norm. After spending three to four years in university and devoting six or seven years of your life to a company, you will hopefully meet the right person and get married. . . .

Historically, in Japan, women have idolized men. They waited on their every whim and desire. Women were educated to perform for their men, to play musical instruments, to sing, to whisper in their ears, and to take care of even their smallest needs. The most famous and highly trained in this profession were the famous Geisha.

In the Japanese offices of today, sometimes it seems not much has changed. The cultural traditions of the sexual roles run deep, and women still feel that it is their duty to tend to the needs of their male counterparts. . . .

It would probably not surprise Dana to learn that other countries are less open to career-oriented women. But Jean's emphasis on the cultural context of work and home usefully problematizes the focus in Dana's paper on the psychological concept of self. To talk about self one cannot really imagine a conceptual space outside of patriarchy. But there is another sense in which Jean's paper could also prove valuable—not for ideas but for what it represents: another woman reflecting critically upon her own experience with discrimination. Is there any reason to keep students like Dana, enrolled in technical institutes that have limited resources for Women's Studies and the Humanities away from students like Jean? Who benefits when papers like Dana's are merely processed and graded, rather than shared or critiqued by students across the campus, the city, or the country?

Dana, I should say, earned a decent grade in the course, but her foray into this subject would not win any awards in a student writing contest, or, I dare say, a decent grade in a more prestigious department. That is, however, the least of my concerns. My point is that by funneling students into models of achievement that are, for all intents and purposes, not within their reach, or not within their goals and objectives, we are not just setting up our students and ourselves for failure, but we are losing an opportunity to establish more meaningful reasons to read, write, and do research in higher education.

It could be argued, without much resistance, of course, that it is not the writing center's job to reconstruct the undergraduate curriculum. Yet writing "centers" are central to nothing if they are not central to students' varied efforts to write their papers in the curriculum. Ignoring what goes on there, ultimately, does not improve upon the lives of student writers. Likewise, as I hope I have also demonstrated, even in this tentative form, real change does not have to translate into top–down curricular reform or large-scale faculty development—two features that characterize the successes and the failures of many WAC movements. Change can be local, student-centered, and exploratory, just like a writing center. However, if change is to be lasting and meaningful, writing centers and computers and composition will need much more than each other. They will need the (refigured) discipline of Composition.

THE IDEA/OLOGY OF THE ELECTRONIC WRITING CENTER

Earlier I described this chapter as an educational fantasy. That, perhaps, was a poor choice of words, if the fantasy refers only to the idea of the electronic writing center. No, the real fantasy is that university communities would see an electronic writing center as a knowledge center; that they would construe this use of other students' papers not as a form of plagiarism—as a term paper warehouse—but as an educational project, a move toward dialogic literacy that knows no boundaries between disciplines, geography, time, and levels of education.

Although I found these texts on the Internet, in undergraduate e-zines, on faculty/course homepages, and through Writing Program web sites, I believe there is a case to be made for one-stop-shopping. Writing centers should play more of an active role in collecting their own students' writings in one, electronic space, using these writings in other tutorials, and developing larger, more visible web sites, perhaps through the National Writing Center Association. "Writing" would no longer only refer to a process or a textual surface but to actual student-writings-in philosophy, history, literature, anthropology, psychology, public policy, environmental geology, and so on. These writings would not be presented to students as models, or exemplars, but as intellectual counterpoint. I imagine a day, in other words, when students can quote other students as they write, connecting their work not just to their professors or classmates but to those writers that have engaged the same subjects, at different times, in different places, in dissimilar conditions.

Ultimately, however, I believe I am asking us to consider much more than a web site or two. I am asking us to reconsider the ways in which the university hails undergraduates as writers and the ways we in writing centers support that hail. I am asking us to scrutinize the reasons why electronic technologies have not been used to link more students together in dialogic partnerships. As Althusser has indicated, ideology is not an illusion but a material practice. Therefore, it is important to locate resistance in pedagogical, curricular, and technological practices, not just in philosophies of teaching or theories of literacy. That is why I have emphasized the intersection of writing centers and computers and composition in this book: both fields are tangible sites in which the Subject of Composition is produced. To Althusser, this Subject is always enmeshed in a larger class struggle, wagered not through violence but through the ISAs. The goal of this struggle is to control the relations of production in the apparatus. Althusser's take on resistance, then, is useful here insofar as it forces us to theorize in practice.

But Bakhtin's innovation on the problem of interpellation, in my view, is equally compelling because he posits the utterance, itself, as a site of resistance. For some students like Katie and Bill the utterance can be surprisingly powerful, even when it is formulated under duress. For other students like Anne and Kee, the internally persuasive utterance might be viewed with suspicion. Discussions about other students' papers, for example, could seem like wandering, off-task activities, even if they are just confined to email. They will ask us, "why do I need to talk about this? What's the point? Will it get me a better grade?" And I sympathize with those responses. Students are busy. They care most about getting those papers written. But are we willing to conclude, then, along with our students, that writing in college really is just an emergency that needs to be taken care of quickly, painlessly, in as few drafts as possible? Are we willing to forfeit dialogic literacy?

Admittedly, the idea of the electronic writing center is just an idea: one part curricular reform, one part pedagogical idea, and several parts hope. Framed the way it is, not upon a sense of crisis but upon a sense of opportunity, I wonder sometimes if the idea even has a chance. There is nothing to suggest that students should write together across course sections, sharing their ideas beyond the isolated "communities" of the classroom or the center; nothing to suggest that academic departments should tolerate collective, interdisciplinary, inquiry by students. There is, in other words, no dire need for an electronic writing center. And this is the reason why it most needs to be built. Within the silence of our complicity, the very possibility of dialogic literacy appears wrong. But it doesn't have to be that way.

5

Computing the Field of Composition

Radical composition teachers must remember that we inherit an oppressive institutional history and a repressive intellectual tradition. We inherit an institutional structure that was created in order to serve as a social and intellectual gatekeeper. It's operational status was and still is grounded in nineteenth-century hopes for literacy, assumptions about who was, and who could become, "an educated person" and about the most efficient ways of fitting people to compete aggressively, if obediently, in a capitalist society. Institution Freshman English has always been a gesture toward general fears of illiteracy among the population at large, fears generated by America's very real class hierarchies. Hence I question the wisdom, as well as the possibility, of turning Freshman English to radical purposes.   — (Crowley, 1991, p. 165)

What I am finally suggesting is that we let our pedagogy emerge out of our discipline rather than let our discipline be ruled by an ill-conceived and rotting pedagogical structure.   — (Goggin, 1995, p. 43)

Here, at the end of this paper, I find myself trying to articulate a position for composition between critical negation and carelessness. Or, to put it another way, I want to try to imagine a way for composition to name a critical project, one that is local, one whose effects will be necessarily limited, but one, still, of significant consequence.   — (Bartholomae, 1996, p. 24)

Although one could argue that the research community in Composition Studies has, to some degree, reframed the terms of literacy instruction in higher education, most notably, through widespread penetration of process theories, one could also argue that, since the main curricular location for literacy instruction remains outside of or somehow prior to meaningful academic work, that the "discipline" of Composition has been purchased at a very high price. I am not just referring to a symbolic price, either. Susan Miller (1991) estimates that, between teaching assignments, textbooks, and administrative costs, approximately "$100 million is spent each year in America on something we might think of as teaching students to write at the college level" (p. 5). It is a suspiciously large investment of resources that ought to rouse more speculation than it does.

Although I have had little to say, throughout this book, about those major expenditures that Miller concerns herself with, I have had plenty to say about the ways that Composition allocates time and money to sustain an ISA of functional literacy in writing centers and computers and composition. While it may be true that, in the grand scheme of things, these fields account for very little of that 100 million dollar investment in literacy, I would maintain that because both fields were created to shoulder the load of functional literacy, or to take "basic" writing problems out of the traditional classroom, these fields are by no means insignificant players in the construction of disciplinarity. In that light, they deserve much more serious consideration, particularly amongst theorists and practitioners who are seeking out new relations of production in the apparatus of literacy, including, but not limited to, those pedagogical, curricular, and technological relations that emphasize what Mary Louise Pratt (1991) calls the arts of the contact zone.

As a form of resistance to the hail of functional literacy, I have therefore foregrounded those moments in the electronic writing center where students can latch onto a centrifugal opening in the subject; those moments where writers can reappropriate authoritative discourses with their own accents and intentions. Admittedly, I have risked quite a bit in the process, namely, the Strategy of Containment and the Rhetoric of Technocentrism. I have also jeopardized the boundaries between writing centers and computers and composition, between both fields and the discipline, between the discipline and the larger constituencies it serves. If this were a confession to a crime, I would now have to come clean: I did all these things with full cognizance of the laws I was breaking. And I would do it again.

How then are we to understand my brazen disregard of the law? Have I simply buried my head under a pillow while the siren of functional literacy wails on in the background? Since I am already in confessional mode, I suppose I could plead guilty to that one, too. But I believe the issue goes beyond me, writing centers, and computers and composition. The issue has to do with the ways we construct the larger discipline. How then are we, in Composition, to make sense of electronic writing spaces that do not respond to that siren wail? How are we to value these spaces, in the context of an ISA that continues to marshal an intimidating array of resources—credit hours, space allocations, salaries and stipends—to produce a much different, monologic literacy? What can the larger discipline of Composition do to make room for dialogic literacy in the writing center?

In suggesting that the discipline ought to issue a new hail, I do not mean to suggest that nothing has been done already to reconceive pedagogical or curricular relations. Nevertheless, if we can see the movement toward networked writing classrooms, for example, as intimations toward the dialogic, we can also see these environments for what they are: thorns in the side of functional literacy. In the next section, I would like to take a look at the research on networked writing in the classroom, in part, because this research has helped call into question the pedagogy of teaching writing and the values of good writing. The objection will be raised, of course that, since classrooms are so different from writing centers, a comparison would be pointless. Yet, as I hope to show below, these methodological differences, though significant, do not cancel out the more provocative finding; that centrifugal openings in the electronic writing classroom are not always met with praise. Understanding the dissonance between dialogic possibility and ideological reality in the classroom, might help us contextualize the larger problem that I have concerned myself with in this book: the problem of implementing dialogic literacy across the curriculum, through bottom–up initiatives such as the email conference or the EWC.

A CHAIN OF SIGNIFIERS OR BETTER ESSAYS?

Though scholars and practitioners in Composition Studies have, since the early days of teaching machines and word processing research, grown skeptical of studies that claim "computers improve writing," the specter of indisputable progress through technology is never far away in Composition Studies. Interestingly enough, though, the question that gets asked about networked writing classrooms is different. There, the focus of attention is not so much on the end result—will networked environments lead students to produce better papers—but on the immediate experience of conferencing. In particular, it has been theorized that networked environments are more egalitarian than traditional classrooms.

Cooper and Selfe (1990), for example, have noted that asynchronous bulletin boards can interrupt standard academic protocol in writing courses by giving students an opportunity to fight the accommodating impulse of the classroom—to be "right," to be "good" and so on—and to develop instead an "internally persuasive discourse" (p. 860). Unlike students in traditional classrooms, students who use asynchronous bulletin boards "dissent not only intellectually but linguistically and stylistically as well—ruling out a strict adherence to formal academic prose warding humor, and poking fun at the gravity with which the subject matter is treated in the classroom" (p. 857).

Barker and Kemp (1990), likewise, have argued that synchronous conferencing works because it facilitates a "pure" interaction between students: through "psychological filtering"—the disappearance, or filtering out of body language and intonation—students and teachers can become liberated from "all the paraphernalia that allows physical context to intrude on and inhibit the pure exchange of ideas" (Barker & Kemp, p. 21), including voice, stature, bearing, and timing. Within synchronous environments, Bump (1990) has also noted that students who generally do not speak in class—who are often depicted as shy or as minorities—find that they do not have to compete for the floor, and hence, more students tend to participate. Such unprecedented freedom to "say anything" curtails the teacher's ability to control discussion, and in this limited sense, networked environments can claim egalitarianism—if by egalitarianism, we simply mean the freedom to write. There is no turn taking in a computer-mediated discussion: Students write their messages whenever they please, and they likewise read what they choose to read. They are not guided through a discussion, held by a teacher's gaze, or challenged to respond immediately to a teacher's questions.

This shift in focus, away from the singular writer toward the dynamics of the negotiating group, suggests a larger shift in Composition toward collaborative models of learning and the social construction of knowledge. Much the same way prewriting dialogue programs were made to embody research in pre-writing, networked environments have been seized upon as physical embodiments of the social. With this alignment, however, there has been some interesting fallout. As Geoffrey Sirc and Thomas Reynolds (1993) pointed out, when students are asked to review each other's drafts online, they tend to "review" the general subject that the writer chose, not so much the actual sentences or phrases that the writer used: They see the text as a spoken utterance, not so much as a "draft" in need of refinement or clarification. Similarly, Faigley (1992) has noted that while students can remember what was said on the network, they can't always remember who said what. This leads them to create an indeterminate, apparently author-less text, or what often feels like an endless scroll of messages. On this point, Anthony DiMatteo (1990) has written, "not only does no one have the final say [online] but even the notion of a *final say* is brought into doubt" (p. 76). Where much of the social turn in composition celebrates the movement toward consensus in a group, these studies imply a movement toward dissensus.

Of course, that movement can be problematic, especially on the receiving end of somebody else's internally persuasive discourse. For example, in the transcript that Joe Janangelo (1991) discussed, a student named Ella, "a first year college student of Soviet extraction" (p. 57), was ostracized from the group because of her conservative opinions on premarital sex and drinking. As well, her heavy Russian accent and other physical traits provoked her classmates, in Janangelo's words "to anonymously humiliate her in public."

> The danger here is that the anonymity of computer-generated text gives writers the option of publishing discourse without taking responsibility for its contents. With no hallmark to identify them, some writers may feel free to speak their minds, even when

they know that they are being offensive or hurtful. Inscribed within the writer's freedom to be both candid and anonymous is the potential to menace others. For me, the possibility that this new anonymity may facilitate the disclosure of a writer's true feelings takes on a darker resonance when it is measured against the abuses of power by irresponsible individuals, and the anxiety experienced by helpless targets of a hostile conversation. (p. 60)

The network, in other words, allowed Janangelo's students to express what they would have otherwise never expressed in his traditional classroom. The problem is not limited to Janangelo, either. A similar incident, perhaps less contentious but no less serious, occurred in Susan Romano's (1993) classroom: One of her Mexican-American students revealed to Romano, off-line, that the best thing about Interchange is that it allowed her to hide her ethnic identity from other students; no one could hear her accent. Romano points out that this use of the network is not very egalitarian. It suggests, to the contrary, a deepening of social divisions whereby minority voices are not so much incorporated onto the network as they are erased or ignored. Though Romano praises this form of interaction for disrupting the teacher-centered classroom, she seems wary, as does Janangelo, of a truly anonymous, free speech forum where *any* discourse—however slanderous or assimilationist—can be used.

On the network, as Lester Faigley (1992) explains, "agency resides in the power of connecting with others and building alliances" (p. 199), and clearly, it is this power of the alliance that allowed Janangelo's students to menace their least favorite student; that allowed Romano's student to connect (unproblematically?) with a white majority; that allowed Cooper and Selfe's students to pursue their own concerns about the academic subjects they were studying; that allowed my students (in the writing center) to reformulate their ideas in voices that could not, or would not likely, be used in their formal, monologic papers, to pursue what I called a Rhetoric of Answerability. It is this same power, however, that surprised Marshall Kremers (1988), who described his first electronic class discussion as a form of class "mutiny," implying in the choice of that word that the captain of the ship—the teacher—had been overthrown by ingrates: "Not only did these students seize control of the LAN, they ignored my attempts to bring them back into line, even to the point of defiance... When their exchanges finally descended into pornography, all I could do was switch off their screens" (p. 72). As DiMatteo says of synchronous conferencing, it is a "protean and unruly discourse" (p. 79) that often releases a "bottled up aggression created by the institutionalization of language" (p. 80).

Though I can certainly sympathize with the predicaments that Kremers, Romano, and Janangelo have highlighted, I cannot help but note how these stories also highlight a deep ambivalence toward dissensus. When given the chance to write outside of the usual constraints, it would seem that some students take pot shots at political consensus. And while it is one thing to allow centrifugal voicings into the classroom, however contentious they may be, it is quite another thing to foreground them in relation to larger, programmatic mandates and the allocation of resources.

Whether we see these electronic forums as potentially menacing or potentially liberating, we cannot help but see them, especially in the context of first year writing programs, as unauthorized forums for writing. Kremers (1993) frames the issue from a student's point of view:

> For many of these students, ENFI (Electronic Networks for Interaction) was not an exciting innovation, but rather a new and empty space into which we threw them without explaining why. Already upset at being placed in a remedial course, they were less than eager to participate in an experiment that had no apparent link to the exit exam. For one thing the ENFI class was disorienting in contrast to the conventional classroom. Why didn't the teacher lecture or lead a discussion? Were the rules for measuring performance the same in both classrooms or were they different for ENFI? If so, what were they? ENFI work seemed not to be graded, but non-ENFI work was. Did that make ENFI work 'play' and the other serious work? (p. 117)

The mere presence of collaboratively produced electronic discourse, he seems to say, forces a comparison not only to the genres of the single-authored, paperbound essay (the term paper, the lab report, the essay), but to the pedagogical values associated with those genres. The indeterminacy of networked "writing," in other words, forces a comparison to the over-determined, highly regulated modes of writing and teaching in the university. The informal, conversational rhythm of electronic discourse—not quite writing, not quite speech—can also challenge us to re-think the gatekeeping function of "writing" in the university, as Geoffrey Sirc and Thomas Reynolds (1993) point out below:

> ENFI exists for us, then, mostly as a counterpoint to the traditional student "imaginary," the standard representation of the student writer. Standard measures of writing quality and traditional measures of metalinguistic ability are increasingly unsatisfying to us because we know they don't fully capture our students' strengths (or weaknesses). Transcripts from an ENFI class become an important classroom text that illustrates how students create meaning, interact, pose questions, offer answers, respond to each other's work as well as their own, and become interested and bored by the classroom enterprise. It is active, living literacy. (p. 155)

Yet it is a literacy that seems to have no function in higher education; a literacy that problematizes that drive toward centripetal discourse; a mode of interaction that does not produce "better essays" but instead calls into question the project of learning how to write essays in the consensual classroom; the promise of upward mobility through (functional) literacy.

BEYOND COMMUNITY

If the networked writing classroom calls into question the promise of functional literacy and the foundations of academic community, it is worth pausing to note how this has occurred. In a networked environment, students no longer have to wait for a teacher to legitimate their efforts at communication. They get instant feedback from their peers. This would seem to be a promising development, but Faigley (1992) suggests that, however we perceive it, this highly interactive rhetorical situation may pose a threat to the modernist assumptions in the discipline:

> While many college English teachers are fascinated about the new possibilities that networked computers bring to the classroom, many others are frightened by the possibilities, and they should be, because much more is at stake than relinquishing some of the teacher's traditional authority. Many see classroom acts of writing, especially writing about the self, as part of a much longer process of intellectual self-realization. Writing about the self is given great importance because it encourages reflection about self-development. This legacy of modernism is challenged by writing on computer networks in general (here I'm speaking of asynchronous as well as synchronous discussions). Networked writing displaces the modernist conception of writing as hard work aimed at producing an enduring object. Acts of networked writing are most often quickly produced, quickly consumed, and quickly discarded. . . . It is also difficult for teachers to maintain a notion of students discovering their authentic selves through writing when student writers try on and exchange identities in electronic discussions, even from one message to the next. (p. 191)

To Faigley, the traditional freshman essay—that "enduring object"—retains a shadowy link to modernism, to meta-narratives, to authority and coherence, to a world that is ordered and preserved through writing. Networked writing, by contrast, suggests a post-modern landscape of competing intentions and a market-driven intertextuality. As well, the disruptions in etiquette, civility, and authority, whether they are perceived positively or negatively by classroom teachers, suggest deeper problems in the promise of community, as it is formulated by Composition to new students entering the university.

"Community," as Joe Harris (1989) has argued, is a "powerful yet ill-defined" notion for understanding academic writing. At times, the term refers to the idea of a speech community—an actual group of speakers in close proximity to one another. Yet at other times, it refers to the idea of an interpretive community—a more distant group of like-minded individuals who share the same values. Both ideas of community are dangerously sentimental, according to Harris, and in many ways represent utopias that are "oddly free of many of the tensions, discontinuities, and conflicts in the sorts of talk and writing that go on everyday in the classrooms and departments of an actual university" (p. 270). Stripped of meaningful tension and conflict, "community" becomes something like a wall and faculty and students become insiders and outsiders, which to Harris seems "both overstated and misleading" (p. 275). What students confront in the university—and, I might add, on the computer network—is not so much an interpretive community or even a speech community, but "several continuous and conflicting discourses" that compete for a students' attention. How, then, are we to help students productively sort through this heteroglossia? How can we marshal our resources to create new scenes for dialogic literacy?

I cannot, unfortunately, imagine the best way to do this, nor do I think there really is such a way. But the question is not limited, in my view, to the technicalities of teaching writing in a classroom or in a writing center. To think beyond the limits of community in Composition is to think beyond the limits of the university, as it has been formulated in this century. "The question," says Bill Readings (1996) in *The University in Ruins*, is "not how to turn the institution into a haven for thought but how to think in an institution whose development tends to make thought more and more difficult" (p. 175). What projects such as dialogic literacy require, it would seem, is an alternative not just to the idea of "community" that underlies so many of our writing programs and classrooms, but an alternative to the "Great Divide" between faculty and students; an alternative to transportable writing skills, learned once and then applied to any situation; in short, an alternative to the ISA of literacy, as it continues to frame our work.

Searching for this alternative won't be easy. But it is not hard to see why it needs to be done, if we are to anticipate, rather than lag behind, the larger changes in the ways higher education relates to its constituencies. The pattern, by now, is familiar enough. The decline in public funding, the commodification of knowledge, and the heavy hand of transnational conglomerates, according to Readings, has made the university "a survivor of the era in which it defined itself in terms of the project of the historical development, affirmation, and inculcation of national culture" (p. 6). Unless we are to become complacent with what he calls "the discourse of Excellence" that frames most university mission statements or complacent with the deadening nostalgia for the community that never was, we will need to rethink the purpose of university education in general and college writing in particular. Debates about the canon, the growth of special studies programs, contests over the status of affirmative action, and other typical features of university life after the 1960s should indicate that the center of the university cannot hold; that the "objectivity" of the meritocracy has given way to the subjectivities of race, gender, class, ideological affiliation, and other forms of identity politics. The end of the Cold War, likewise, has signaled the end of massive public funding to higher education and a concurrent rise in funding by the private sector. To Readings (1996), however, none of this indicates failure so much as the end of an era:

> The University no longer has to safeguard and propagate national culture, because the nation-state is no longer the major site at which capital reproduces itself. Hence, the idea of national culture no longer functions as an external referent toward which all of the efforts of research and teaching are directed. The idea of national culture no longer provides an overarching ideological meaning for what goes on in the University, and as a result, what exactly gets taught or produced matters less and less. (p. 13)

Even a cursory glance at the incoherence of general education programs and the fragmentation between and within the disciplines suggests that Readings is—if not right on target—right on track. When we consider that the university fell into ruins at the same time that Composition rose from the ashes, we are left with a most unpromising conclusion: Composition has sustained the idea of community at a time when community has become untenable. The functional ability to communicate with others, transparently, as it were, in the "German Idealist fantasy of the Greek polis" (p. 190) is not provisionally but fundamentally flawed. The historical university has not provided a coherent, egalitarian space for the exchange of information and the sustenance of "community." Rather, it has overwhelmed the subject of university education—over-determined "him" as a neutral, free, autonomous learner. It is this "community" that the students in this book have struggled to understand, with varying degrees of interest and success, this "community" that has assiduously separated domain content from rhetorical process, and this "community" that first year writing programs continue to offer to new students. To speak of community in relation to the university is to speak of a place that is strangely and suspiciously at peace with its role in the culture. Toward what end do we sustain this fiction for our students? Toward what end do we sustain it for ourselves?

What I am looking for, instead, is a dissenual "community" where we can, as Readings advises, "think the social bond without recourse to a unifying idea, whether of culture or the state" (p. 191); to practice a form of reading and writing that strengthens, rather than weakens, our connections with each other. I believe such an alternative exists, at least potentially, in the idea of the electronic writing center. I also believe that the premise is good enough to warrant much more than a fraction of that 100 million dollars that Miller talks about. But I wouldn't want to put a price tag on it.

Appendix

African-American Poetry As Catalyst for Exploring Discrimination

---

A TEACHING GUIDE FOR A FOUR-WEEK UNIT ON POETRY
AND DISCRIMINATION FOR JUNIOR AND SENIOR HIGH
SCHOOL STUDENTS

Poetry and Discrimination

Why Talk About Discrimination?

This is a teaching manual for a four-week unit that utilizes African-American poetry as a vehicle for classroom discourse on the subject of discrimination. The activities are best employed in a cooperative learning, student-centered classroom, in which the teacher serves as facilitator for active student discussions. The lesson plans that follow are designed to help students recognize that they already have a relationship to discrimination—that all have felt first hand its sting, or witnessed its sting, or inflicted its sting. This unit provides an opportunity for students to examine and share their own prejudices and painful experiences with discrimination because HUMAN SURVIVAL, BROTHER AND SISTERHOOD, DEPEND ON IT. As Martin Luther King stated, "We can choose to walk the high road of human brotherhood or to tread the low road of man's inhumanity to man." ("Where Do We Go from Here?" (Stride Toward Freedom)

There is not one right or perfect age at which to begin discussing discrimination. My kindergartener watched the moving PBS special for kids on AIDS featuring Magic Johnson. When she saw the little girl break down, crying and being comforted by Johnson, she felt very sad. I asked her, "Could you play with that little girl...or with any kid who has AIDS?" Her honest five-year-old-not-yet-in-kindergarten answer was, "I don't know. Could I?"

As a loving mother trying to educate my own about something scary, such as AIDS, I reassured her, "Yes, honey. You can play with a kid who has AIDS. You cannot catch it from playing with somebody. You could share a soda, play dolls, play ball, etc." My daughter was greatly relieved. What she doesn't know is that she has met adults and played with kids living with AIDS. There will be a time for full disclosure, but we were trapped by THE SECRET being guarded by the children's parents and our desire that they first experience these kids as kids first, not kids defined or qualified by something.

University at Albany Professor Richard Read's understanding of disability as a human-engineered construct, a relationship outside the self, is applied to the working definition of discrimination, asserting that it, too, is a relationship between a person and his goals, needs, opportunities. Just as disability does not reside in the individual who has a functional impairment, discrimination doesn't reside in the person or organization that discriminates, nor in the victim, even though on a personal level the practitioner of discrimination may harbor judgement, prejudice, fear, or ignorance in his heart. The person victimized by the discrimination has feelings as well, but the effect is that the discrimination is a barrier between the victim and her opportunities. Understanding, self-awareness, enlightened attitudes, improved communication skills, and changed behavior are all resources to help tear down the barriers.

Discrimination is not an academic subject. It is a human subject. Today our schools, community human service organizations and churches offer prevention education programs designed to prevent substance abuse, teenage pregnancy, and sexually transmitted diseases. These programs react to the BIG RISKS preying upon our children, assuming that we can, by early intervention and programming, prevent tomorrow's problems. A Prevention Education Specialist once told me, not completely joking, that his job was to prevent education.

Something is missing amidst all the dispersal of information designed to save the next generation. Yes, there are some innovative programs, such as the employment of Viola Spolin's Theatre Games to nurture self-esteem, creativity, and self-expression. Such projects go a lot further than the Just Say No campaign. What is missing, though, are basics to human communication. Talking. Listening. Responding. Identifying. Students talk incessantly. But what are they sharing that breaks down the human-engineered walls of prejudice and discrimination?

The single most important thing we can do for humanity--brotherhood and sisterhood--is learn something about each other. We do this by taking the risk to share ourselves and by actively listening. We need to talk with, not at. The greatest threat to humanity is our lack of understanding for one another.

The University at Albany has a guiding credo called "The Principles of a Just Community." I have to ask, "What is it to be a member of a growing, creating community whose eyes are set on the prize of justice?" I support the "Principles," but my everyday experience informs me that the goal is in sight, but not necessarily in hand. I do have to wonder what it is about me that fights for civil rights, why it is I identify as strongly as I do with those who have been oppressed and discriminated against? Why do I advocate for myself? Others?

I guess the ability to advocate for oneself is something that must be passed on. What else I can tell you—I was born in 1960. The following prose poem may not speak to all born in 1960, but here is what it was like to be me born in 1960.

The TV news is always on in my house. I know Walter and Dan real well. The first time I ever saw her cry, my mother explained, "The President Died," and all I could figure was, he must be an important guy. I watched the procession on the news, and for years was convinced I had seen the murdered president's actual nose. Everynight, we get the number dead and the number wounded. I don't know how far away Vietnam is, but so far it seems pretty far except those pictures are in my livingroom. My babysitter cries because her boyfriend's number was the bad kind. Dad drags us to silent candlelight vigils, Sundays, on the green in Sharon. This is my church. There is no music. If there are prayers, I cannot hear them. Martin Luther King is on the news a lot, I know his voice. My parents argue about him all the time. What he says sends a crawling chill up my legs--a good kind of chill, like when grandpa reads my favorite poems, or Handel's Messiah my atheist father plays over and over on the record player. When I hear King preach, I think he's making it better so maybe there won't be anymore Vietnams. He talks about a future for his children. I am a kid and I want a future. There's a war in my house, only no dead. Outside my house, elsewhere in America, more assasinations. The message is clear: if you act for change you get killed.

I have to link my need to fight for justice with those early and formative years. I link them to surviving the battlefield of an actively alcoholic and sometimes violent home. I remember my little, differently-abled kid, who sought school for refuge, but fell through a lot of cracks. A kid whose deficits glared, but whose assets rarely got to shine.

Poetry by-passed the deficits, and let the assets out to play. My experience has shown me that people either really enjoy poetry, or treat it like some inaccessible alien art form that requires multiple languages for deciphering. I want poetry to be available. I believe strongly in poetry's transformational effects on the heart, mind, and sou--lif the reader is a willing partner. My job, as teacher, is not only to demonstrate that poetry is accessible, but to allow it to work its transformation/empowerment in my students.

Poetics is the art, craft, and mechanics of writing. One goal was to, as much as possible, allow the voices, wisdom, and experience of African-American teacher/writers, such as Langston Hughes and Countee Cullen, and Audre Lord shape this guide. The wealth of black poetry allows the students to look first at discrimination through the window of race. Since racial discrimination is a dominent theme in African-American poetry, it will serve as a kind of big picture window view of discrimination. Throughout the unit, there will be ample opportunity to transfer insights gained, to look at discrimination through another window, such as discrimination against those with functional impairments, the gay/lesbian population, immigrants, the elderly, the poor, etc.

We need to be ourselves first. Therein lies the magic blueprint for creating a place within where justice can dwell, from which we can clean house, ridding our hearts of the fears, misconceptions, and misunderstandings that separate us from our brothers and sisters. The Christian Church (as well as other faiths) offers that opportunity, but Christ's teachings are not appropriate in public schools. There has to be a secular way for educators to exorcise the disease of prejudice and liberate truth from the souls we teach.

THE POETICS OF DISCRIMINATION COURSE OBJECTIVES

This unit is designed for multiple uses. First, it can be used for the express purpose of studying poetry and the language used to talk about how poems work. Second, this course can offer an alternative program for February, Black History Month. As such, it offers an opportunity for students to apply the works of African-American poets to their lives. Third, it provides an outside the self vantage point from which to gently but directly challenge students' thinking and to encourage discourse on the subject of discrimination. The objectives of the course are:

1. To help students understand that no one is immune to prejudice; prejudice has victims and perpetrators. At one time or another, nearly all have either been its victims or harbored its bad seed, more often both.
    a. Prejudice has more to do with fear and ignorance than it does with color, nationality, or creed.
    b. Honest examination of our own experience with prejudice can help us understand ourselves and others better.
2. To create cooperative learning experiences in which the role of the teacher is facilitator and the students learn from each other's experiences.
3. To better acquaint high school students with the African-American poetry: the sad reality is that thirty years after Langston Hughes was commonly taught in high school English classes, the gradualism that provoked the late Justice Thurgood Marshall to say, "...ninety years is gradual enough..." is still witnessed in the lack of, or minimal inclusion of African-American authors in high school English classes.

4. To begin to see the relationship between being disabled and being disadvantaged. Once this link is made, it makes the case for understanding discrimination as a relationship outside an individual, a human constructed relationship between an individual and opportunity, between an individual and his or her goals. c.f. Professor Richard Read, author of the Handbook for Microcomputing and Disability, states that "

5. To create learning situations in which students can see that although the roots of prejudice are in ignorance, fear, and insecurity, that discrimination man-made. That which is constructed can be deconstructed! Students will discover what they can do to effect changes on the inside...and the outside.

6. To provide an opportunity to examine and apply the language of poetry and poetics.

SUMMARY OF GOALS

The goal is to encourage students to take risks sharing themselves with their peers in a safe, cooperative learning setting; to allow students to apply their life experience to the works by African-American poets, and conversely, to allow the poetry of African-Americans to speak to the students' hearts, challenge their minds, and empower their daily life.

WEEK ONE: Sharing Ourselves and Our Stories

"Nothing that happpens to us is unimportant..."
--Madeleine L'Engle

"This Class...is going to write a poem."
--Countee Cullen

The working vocabulary for Week One is:

civil rights
construct
conversational
deconstruction
disability
disadvantaged
discrimination
free verse
functional impairment
ignorance
image
prejudice

racial discrimination
tone
victim
victimizer
witness

LESSON ONE: MONDAY

Framework/Advance Organizers: Read's Definition
Since discrimination, like disability, is a human-constructed relationship that doesn't reside within an individual but does effectively create barriers, the object for this lesson is to recall, explore, and share a situation in which the student had an experience with discrimination; the hope is to make the connection between what was felt on the inside, and what behavior was manifested on the outside, and to try on another's story.

Common Language
  The above list of vocabulary for the first week's lessons contains language used to talk about poetry, and language used to talk about discrimination. A working vocabulary for the study of poetry is needed for all—for ninth graders, many may be new terms not previously encountered in their study of literature. Review is essential for older students, even if these lessons are used for undergraduates, because: 1) students forget, 2) students need opportunities to apply the language of poetry, not just rehearse definitions for exams, 3) preparation of students is often uneven, and 4) poetics is about how a poem is made and how it works. It is all too easy for students to slip into the vague world of "I feel" when talking about poetry: this is not invalid when confronting and sharing experiences with prejudice, but "I feel" doesn't indicate whether a poem is a sonnet, free verse, blank verse, etc. Likewise, students need language to talk about discrimination.
  Students need to arrive at and agree on definitions of the above vocabulary list before the lessons can progress. While the definitions of some of these words can be looked up in a dictionary, and to a large extent are NOT debatable, the concept of prejudice being rooted in fear, isolation and ignorance AND the understanding of discrimination as a human construct, a
  relationship, a barrier (c.f. Read, disability) must be the foundation of subsequent inquiry. It is best to start with an explanation of Prof. Read's understanding of disability as a construct residing outside the individual, because this concept will be quickly applied to the discussion of racial discrimination. At least ten minutes should be spent going over the vocabulary; a handout with working definitions could be passed out, but it is important that students understand and have an opportunity to question and debate. If the class discussion is especially fruitful, up to fifteen minutes could be spent, but the debate should be tabled for later in the week, as the class needs the exercises to help them discover and try on new meanings. The teacher is not a know-er who can just handout meaning and expect the students to

digest and regurgitate it. In order to encourage the students to own the vocabulary is to give each week, a list of the words with room to write the definitions, and ask them to complete and turn in on Friday.

Encourage the students to borrow from class discussions/notes rather than simply copy from the dictionary.

Readings/In-class activity:

Ask different students to read Countee Cullen's "Incident" and "Scottsboro, Too, Is Worth Its Song" ALSO: (as a prose poem) "I Want So Many Things" from the play, A Raisin in the Sun by Lorraine Hansberry (this will take two readers.) It does not hurt for the teacher to read one of the parts or selections, to model ways in which poetry can be recited, but it is important to give students a chance to practice, also. These selections will only take a few minutes to read, but it is important to hear each selection read at least twice, by different readers. This allows more to participate, and offers students a sampling of possible ways to read or recite the works.

"I Want..." is selected because it is dialogue from a play, and not only does it have the conversational tone required for the storytelling and writing exercises that follows, but it also works as a prose poem. "Scottsboro, Too..." is included to pass on the inspiration, it is encouragemen--tand challenge--from teacher Countee Cullen to the students assembled. "Incident" is an example--simple, direct, honest--of the kind of recollection that will be asked of the students in the following storytelling exercise. Each passage should be explored for meaning, tone, structure, image, etc. Motivation and feeling are also worthy to explore, especially with the dialogue from Raisin in the Sun.

Assignment: Ask the students to begin a journal devoted to this four-week unit. Request 15 minutes/day, their choice related to the subject matter of poetry and discrimination. Journals should be turned in weekly. Assure that entries will be confidential, if so desired by the student.

WEEK ONE, LESSON TWO: TUESDAY

Framework/Advance Organizers

The quotes given by L'Engle and Cullen at the end of this unit should be written on the board before the students come into the classroom. It would be helpful if the three works read and discussed in the previous class could be enlarged and printed to display on walls of the class, where their image serves to triggor the students memory and prod their thinking. After whatever administrative duties, refer to the works, and ask if the students had any further thought or questions about them. Perhaps "Incident" could be reread, aloud, by the teacher. Call attention to the quotes on the board.

In Class Activity:

Students will pair up with someone in class they do NOT know well, or who they would like to get to know better. Each relates to the other an experience, preferably from childhood, (ages 10-14 are often very fruitful, but earlier or more recent is OK) in which they witnessed discrimination, were discriminated against, felt they had been judged on the basis of race, creed, or functional impairment. The students pair off, and each in the pair tells his/her story. The partner, receiver of the story, relates it back to make sure details, sentiments, etc are accurate. This is a great beginning exercise for this unit, because students get to "try on" their partners' stories. Some embellishment is bound to occur, because story telling is entertainment and because there has not been much time to memorize or rehearse the story. What is important is that each student strive to be honest to the integrity and feeling of the story, even if some details are missed. This is why the story is fed back, to verify that the partner "got it." During the feedback, the original owner of the story can correct details that are important to him/her.

Then give the students the remaining fifteen or so minutes to write down, simple prose, no mind to grammar, punctuation, etc. the partner's story. They must work quickly and carefully to capture the essence of the story, as many details as possible, in writing to bring to the next class. The purpose is to make sure they do not forget the heart of the story, and its important details. They may be used as a reminder at home, before class, etc. IT IS IMPERATIVE that these prose pieces do not become cheat sheets to read aloud during the storytelling opportunities: NO NOTES, NO NOTES, NO NOTES: WING IT!

Assignments:
1. 15 minutes of journal writing in response to class.
2. Each student is to write a poem, up to 12-14 lines, telling their partner's story. The students should strive to make their language fluid, from the guts of one to the guts of another, not letting anything fall flat. The tone should be conversational. Students should not worry about rhyme or meter; free verse offers the best chance for a conversational tone. Poetic license is granted because the student poet cannot create without injecting some of him/herself into the work—in trying on another's story, ownership is, at least, temporarily passed from the tell-or to the tell-ee. This temporary ownership is to be respected, not abused. It is possible to have some creative liberty and stay true to the story. These will be collected the following class and read aloud, by their authors, later in the week.
3. Ask students to wear loose, comfortable clothing to the next TWO classes.

WEEK ONE, LESSONS THREE & FOUR: WEDNESDAY AND THURSDAY

Framwork/Advance Organizers:
It's story time! Shove all the desks/desk chairs towards the back before or as the students come in (they can help!) Ask everyone to sit down in a circle on the floor and kick back. Take a few minutes, to lead the class in some basic stretches, warm-

ups, including theatre vocal exercises (see Appendices.) Or, ask a student to do like-wise. (Suggestions for format in Appendix ___.) Save administrative business for last five minutes of class, if at all possible.

In-Class Activity:

Announce that it is time for storytelling, and ask each storyteller to try to keep it under three minutes. The teacher must decide if all will remain sitting while telling their partners' stories, or if each will "stand and deliver." There are advantages to both. Standing probably allows for the story to be performed, but it can cause stiff necks and may serve to pull the teller away from the group. There is a greater chance for conversational language if both teller and tell-ees are at same height. (If students refuse to sit on floor, return to desks, and request each to stand at front of class when it is his/her turn. This provides more of a pre-cenium/audience rapport, more opportunity for performing the stories, but less conversational tone.) This works best when the students are sitting in a circle, facing each other.

Aproximately 5-7 pairs will have time to tell the partner's story before the end of class. Those remaining will have their opportunities the next day. Classes with over twenty four students will probably need Thursday for each to get a turn. A student should be given the job of timer, and handed a watch.

After three minutes, the timer should announce "time." If no student wants this job, the teacher is elected!

Assignments for Wednesday:

1. Continued journal entries in response to class work and remind students to be working on their own dictionaries or lexicons for the vocabulary sheets. Remind them that the point is not just a definition of the word, but the application of that vocabulary word to their experience.

2. Reading: Arna Bontemps, "A Black Man Talks of Reaping," and "Reconnaissance." Poems should be xeroxed, so that students can underline images. Students should pose questions about these poems in their journals.

3. Wear comfortable clothes again for Thursday's class, and bring journals with their questions about Bontemps' poems.

Assignments for Thursday:

1. Continued journal entries and vocabulary sheets, to be turned in on Friday.

2. STUDY FOR IN-CLASS WRITING: One way to understand Cullen's "Scottsboro, Too..." is that it serves as challenge, as plea, for another generation to carry on, for more voices to cry out, for young people not to forget the past. It challenges young poets to carry on. Pretend this poem is a letter from Cullen to you. What is he asking you to do? How do you respond to his challenge? Make some notes in your journals, and bring them with texts, xeroxes, notes to class to use in open-book in-class writing exercise.

WEEK ONE: FRIDAY

In-class writing, see Thursday's assignment. Encourage students to proof-read or edit. Specific questions taken from assignment from Thursday:

1. Pretend this is poem is a letter from Cullen to you.
2. What is he asking you to do? How can you carry the message? What message is he asking you to carry? How do you respond to his challenge? What are simple, reachable goals or tasks you can do to meet the challenge?
3. Can you find any connections between the story you told and what you hear Cullen asking in "Scottsboro, Too..." ? If so, please show where in your story and where in the poem you find the connection(s). (You may look for connections in both your own story and your partner's story.)

Notes

---

[1] The term "technocentrism" was first used by Seymor Pappert (1987) in his article "Computer criticism vs. technocentric thinking" published by *Educational Researcher*. It was then picked up by Gail Hawisher (1989) in the article "Research and recommendations for computers and composition" published in *Critical Perspectives on Computers and Composition*. The phrase "Rhetoric of Technocentrism" is based, in part, on these sources and on Hawisher and Selfe's (1991) article "The rhetoric of technology," published in *College Composition and Communication*.

[2] A note on mechanics: Although I have presented this portion of my exchange with Anne as a back-and-forth dialogue, readers should keep in mind that our exchange did not take place in real time: a question asked on a Tuesday might not receive an answer until Thursday. In between Tuesday and Thursday, other questions or comments might have been made. To provide each other with some continuity, we made liberal use of the reply key, often appropriating each other's email into the new post. In order to make the session readable in this context, however, I have excluded email header information, and I have condensed the repetitious material.

References

Almasy, R. (1982). The nature of writing-laboratory instruction for the developing student. In M. Harris (Ed.), *Tutoring writing: A sourcebook for writing labs* (pp. 13–20). Glenview, IL: Scott, Foresman and Co.

Althusser, L. (1971). *Lenin and philosophy.* New York: Monthly Review Press.

Arms, V. (1983). Creating and recreating. *College Composition and Communication, 34,* 355–358.

Bakhtin, M. (1981). *The dialogic imagination: Four essays.* Austin, TX: University of Texas Press.

Bakhtin, M. (1990). *Art and answerability: Early philisophical essays by M.M. Bakhtin.* Austin, TX: University of Texas Press.

Bamberg, B. (1982). The writing lab and the composition class: A fruitful collaboration. In M. Harris (Ed.). *Tutoring writing: A sourcebook for writing labs* (pp. 179–185). Glenview, IL: Scott, Foresman and Co.

Barker, T. (1984). The English microlab registry: A tool for researchers in computers and composition. *Computers and Composition, 1*(3), 13.

Barker, T. (1990). Computers and the instructional context. In D. Holdstein & C. Selfe (Eds.), *Computers and writing: Theory, research, practice* (pp. 7–17). New York: Modern Language Association.

Barker, T., & Kemp, F. (1990). Network theory: A postmodern pedagogy for the writing classroom. In C. Handa (Ed.), *Computers and community* (pp. 1–23). Portsmouth, NH: Boynton/Cook.

Bartholomae, D. (1985). Inventing the university. In M. Rose (Ed.) *When a writer can't write: Studies in writer's block and other composing problems* (pp. 273–285). New York: Guilford Press.

Bartholomae, D. (1996). What is composition and (if you know what that is) why do we teach it? In L. Bloom, D. Daiker, & E. White (Eds.), *Composition in the twenty-first century: Crisis and change* (pp. 11–28). Carbondale, IL Southern Illinois University Press.

Belenky, M. F., Clinchy, B. M., Goldberger, N. R., & Tarule, J. M. (1986). *Women's ways of knowing: The development of self, voice, and mind.* New York: Basic Books

Bendetti, P., & DeHart, N. (1996). *Forward through the rearview mirror: Reflections on and by Marshall McLuhan.* Cambridge, MA: Massachusetts Institute of Technology.

Berlin, J. (1996). *Rhetoric, poetics, and cultures: Refiguring college English studies.* Urbana, IL: National Council of Teachers of English.

Blythe, S. (1997). Networked computers + writing centers = ? Thinking about networked computers in writing center practice. *The Writing Center Journal, 17*(2), 89–110.

Breininger, L., & Portch, S. (1983). A visit to professor Cram: Attractive computer learning. *College Composition and Communication, 34,* 358–360.

Brown, A. (1990). Coping with computers in the writing center. *The Writing Lab Newsletter, 15*(4), 13–15.

Bruffee, K. (1984). Collaborative learning and the 'conversation of mankind.' *College English, 46,* 635–652

Bullock, R., Schuster, C., & Trimbur, J. (1991). *The politics of writing instruction: Postsecondary.* Portsmouth: Boynton/Cook.

Bump, J. (1990). Radical changes in class discussion using networked computers. *Computers and the Humanities, 24,* 49–65.

Burns, H. (1979). Stimulating rhetorical invention in English composition through computer-assisted instruction. *Dissertation Abstract International, 40,* 3734A. (University Microfilms No. 79–28268)

Burns, H. (1984). Recollections of first-generation computer-assisted prewriting. In W. Wresch (Ed.), *The computer in composition instruction: A writer's tool* (pp. 15–33). Urbana, IL: NCTE.

Carino, P. (1992). What do we talk about when we talk about our metaphors: A cultural critique of clinic, lab, and center. *The Writing Center Journal, 13*(1), 31–41.

Clark, K., & Holquist, M. (1984). *Mikhail Bakhtin.* Cambridge: Harvard University Press.

Clark, I. (1988). Collaboration and ethics in writing center pedagogy. *The Writing Center Journal, 9*(1), 3–12.

Cohen, M., & Lanham, R. (1984). HOMER: Teaching style with a microcomputer. In W. Wresch (Ed.), *The computer in composition instruction: A writer's tool* (pp. 83–90). Urbana, IL: National Council of Teachers of English.

Committee on CCCC Language Statement. (1974). Students' right to their own language. *College Composition and Communication 15,* 1–32.

Connors, R. (1983). Composition studies and science. *College English, 45,* 1–20.

Coogan, D. (1994). Towards a rhetoric of online tutoring. *The Writing Lab Newsletter, 19*(1), 3–5.

Coogan, D. (1995). E-mail tutoring, a new way to do new work. *Computers and Composition, 12,* 171–181.

Cooper, M. (1994). Dialogic learning across disciplines. *Journal of Advanced Composition, 14*(2), 531–545.

Cooper, M., & Selfe, C. (1990). Computer conferences and learning: Authority, resistance, and internally persuasive discourse. *College English, 52,* 847–869.

Cox, D. (1988). Developing software for freshman composition: Sentence patterns. *Collegiate Microcomputer, 6*(2), 161–164.

Crowley, S. (1991). A personal essay on freshman English. *PRE/TEXT, 12*(3–4), 155–178

Crump, E. (1995, March). *Writing centers as provocateurs.* Paper presented at the Conference on College Composition and Communication, Washington, DC.

Daiute, C. (1983). The computer as stylus and audience. *College Composition and Communication, 34,* 134–145.

Dalgish, G. (1987). Randomization and creative open-endedness in English as a second language software. *Collegiate Microcomputer, 5*(1), 66–69.

Daniell, B. (1986). Against the great leap theory of literacy. *PRE/TEXT, 7*(3–4), 181–193.

DiMatteo, A. (1990). Under erasure: A theory for interactive writing in real time. *Computers and Composition, 7*(S.I.), 71–84.

Ede, L. (1989). Writing as a social process: A theoretical foundation for writing centers? *The Writing Center Journal, 9*(2), 3–15.

Elbow, P. (1973). *Writing without teachers.* New York: Oxford University Press.

Faigley, L. (1992). *Fragments of rationality: Postmodernity and the subject of composition.* Pittsburgh: University of Pittsburgh Press.

Farrell, E. (1967). *English, education, and the electronic revolution.* Champaign, IL: National Council of Teachers of English.

Farrell, T. (1978). Differentiating writing from talking. *College Composition and Communication, 29,* 207–214.

Feenberg, A. (1989). *The written world: On the theory and practice of computer conferencing.* In R. Mason and A. Kaye (Eds.), Mindweave, (pp. 22–39). New York: Pergamon Press.

Flower, L. (1979). Writer-based prose: A cognitive basis for problems in writing. *College English, 41*(1), 19–37.

Flower, L. (1994). *The construction of negotiated meaning: A social cognitive theory of writing.* Carbondale and Edwardsville: Southern Illinois University Press.

Forehand, G. (1987). Development of a computerized diagnostic testing program. *Collegiate Microcomputer, 5*(1), 55–59.

Forrest, J. (1998). The office lady in Japan. *Intertext, 6* [online]. Path: http://wrt.syr.edu/wrt/pub/intertext/VI/forrest.html.

Freed, S. (1989). Subjectivity in the tutorial session: How far can we go? *The Writing Center Journal, 10*(1), 39–43.

Geisler, C. (1994). *Academic literacy and the nature of expertise: Reading, writing, and knowing in academic philosophy.* Hillsdale, NJ: Erlbaum.

Gillam, A. (1991). Writing center ecology: A Bakhtinian perspective. *The Writing Center Journal, 11*(2), 3–11.

Goffman, E. (1959). *The presentation of self in everyday life.* New York: Doubleday.

Goffman, E. (1961). *Asylums: Essays on the social situation of mental patients and other inmates.* New York: Doubleday.

Goffman, E. (1967). *Interaction ritual: Essays in face-to-face behavior.* Chicago: Aldine Publishing Co.

Goggin, M. D. (1995). The disciplinary instability of composition. In J. Petraglia (Ed.), *Reconceiving writing, rethinking writing instruction* (pp. 27–48). Mahwah, NJ: Erlbaum.

Grimm, N. (1996). Rearticulating the work of the writing center. *College Composition and Communication, 47*(4), 523–548.

Haas, C. (1996). *Writing technology: Studies on the materiality of literacy.* Mahwah, NJ: Erlbaum.

Haas, C., & Neuwirth, C. (1994). Writing the technology that writes us. In C. Selfe & S. Hilligoss (Eds.), *Literacy and computers: The complications of teaching and learning with technology* (pp. 319–335). New York: Modern Language Association.

Hairston, M. (1982). The winds of change: Thomas Kuhn and the revolution in the teaching of writing. *College Compositoin and Communication, 33*, 76–88.

Haring-Smith, T., Hawkins, N., Morrison, E., Stern, L., & Tatu, R. (1985). *A guide to writing programs: Writing centers, peer tutoring programs, and writing across the curriculum.* Glenview IL: Scott, Foresman and Co.

Harkin, P., & Schilb, J. (1991). *Contending with words: Composition and rhetoric in a postmodern age.* New York: Modern Language Association.

Harris, J. (1989). The idea of community in the study of writing. *College Composition and Communication, 40,* 11–22.

Harris, M. (1981). Process and product: Dominant models for writing centers. In P. Brooks & T. Hawkins (Eds.), *Improving writing skills* (pp. 1–8). San Francisco: Jossey-Bass, Inc.

Harris, M. (1982). *Tutoring writing: A sourcebook for writing labs.* Glenview, IL: Scott, Foresman and Company.

Harris, M. (1990). What's up and what's in: Trends and traditions in writing centers. *The Writing Center Journal, 11*(1), 15–26.

Harris, M. (1995). Talking in the middle: Why writers need writing tutors. *College English, 57*(1), 27–42.

Hawisher, G. (1989). Research and recommendations for computers and composition. In G. Hawisher & C. Selfe (Eds.) *Critical perspectives on computers and composition instruction* (pp. 44–69). New York: Teachers College Press.

Hawisher, G. (1987). Research update: Writing and word processing. *Computers and Composition, 5*(2), 7–25.

Hawisher, G., & Selfe, C. (1991) *Evolving perspectives on computers and composition studies: Questions for the 1990s.* Urbana, IL: National Council of Teachers of English.

Hawisher, G., & Selfe, C. (1991). The rhetoric of technology and the electronic writing class. *College Composition and Communication, 42,* 55–65.

Hawkins, T. (1980). Intimacy and audience: The relationship between revision and the social dimension of peer tutoring. *College English, 42,* 64–68.

Herzberg, B. (1991). Composition and the politics of the curriculum. In R. Bullocks, J. Trimbur, & Charles S. (Eds.), *The politics of writing instruction: Postsecondary* (pp. 97–118). Portsmouth, NH: Boynton/Cook.

Holdstein, D. (1983). The WRITEWELL series. *Computers and Composition, 1*(1), 7.

Hook, M. (1987). The passive voice. *Collegiate Microcomputer, 5*(1), 36–40.

Hubbuch, S. (1988). A tutor needs to know the subject matter to help a student with a paper: __Agree __disagree __not sure. *The Writing Center Journal, 8*(2), 23–30.

Janangelo, J. (1991). Technopower and technoppression: Some abuses of power and control in computer-assisted writing environments. *Computers and Composition, 9*(1), 47–62.

Johnson, J. (1998). Women and the confederacy. *coyotE: An interdisciplinary, undergraduate journal, 1*(1) [online]. Path: http://192.55.228.48/~ejournal/projects/jjohnson.html.

Joyner, M. (1991). The writing conference and the textuality of power. *The Writing Center Journal, 12*(1), 90–100.

Kaplan, N. (1991). Ideology, technology, and the future of writing instruction. In G. Hawisher and C. Selfe (Eds.), *Evolving perspectives on computers and composition studies: Questions for the 1990s* (pp. 11–42). Urbana, IL: National Council of Teachers of English.

Kellog, R. (1989). Idea processors: Computer aids for planning and composing text. In B. Britton & Shawn G. (Eds.), *Computer writing environments: Theory research and design* (pp. 57–92). Hillsdale, NJ: Erlbaum.

Kelly, L. (1980). One-on-one, Iowa City style: Fifty years of individualized writing instruction. *The Writing Center Journal, 1*(1), 4–21.

Kemp, F. (1987). The user-friendly fallacy. *College Composition and Communication, 38,* 32–39.

Kemp, F. (1992). Who programmed this? Examining the instructional attitudes of writing-support software. *Computers and Composition, 10*(1), 9–24.

Kiefer, K., & Selfe, C. (1983). Letter from the editors. *Computers and Composition, 1*(1), 4.

Kiefer, K., & Smith, C. (1984). Improving students' revising and editing: The writer's workbench system. In W. Wresch (Ed.), *The computer in composition instruction: A writer's tool* (pp. 65–82). Urbana, IL: National Council of Teachers of English.

Kinkead, J. (1987). Computer conversations: E-mail and writing instruction. *College Composition and Communication, 38,* 337–341.

Kinkead, J. (1988). The electronic writing tutor. *The Writing Lab Newsletter, 13*(4), 4–5.

Kinkead, J., & Harris, J. (1993). *Writing centers in context: Twelve case studies.* Urbana, IL: National Council of Teachers English.

Kirkpatrick, C. (1981). The case for autotutorial materials. In P. Brooks & T. Hawkins (Eds.), *Improving writing skills* (pp. 15–24). San Francisco: Jossey-Bass, Inc.

Kitzhaber, A. (1990). *Rhetoric in American colleges, 1850–1900.* Dallas, TX: Southern Methodist University Press.

Klem, E., & Moran, C. (1991). Computers and instructional strategies in the teaching of writing. In G. Hawisher & C. Selfe (Eds.), *Evolving perspectives on computers and composition studies: Questions for the 1990s* (pp. 132–149). Urbana, IL: National Council of Teachers of English.

Knoblauch, C. (1984). The current-traditional paradigm: Neither current, nor traditional, nor a paradigm. Paper presented at the meeting of the *Modern Langugage Association,* Washington, DC.

Knoblauch, C., & Brannon, L. (1984). A philisophical persepective on writing centers and the teaching of writing. In G. Olson (Ed.), *Writing centers: Theory and administration* (pp. 36–47). Urbana, IL: National Council of Teachers English.

Knoblauch, C., & Brannon, L. (1993). *Critical teaching and the idea of literacy.* Portsmouth, NH: Boynton/Cook Publishers.

Kremers, M. (1988). Adams Sherman Hill meets ENFI: An inquiry and a retrospective. *Computers and Composition, 5,* 69–77.

Kremers, M. (1993). Student authority and teacher freedom: ENFI at New York Institute of Technology. In B. Bruce, J. Peyton, & T. Batson (Eds.), *Network-based classrooms: Promises and realities* (pp.113–123). New York: Cambridge University Press.

Kuhn, T. (1962). *The structure of scientific revolutions.* Chicago: University of Chicago Press.

Lassner, P. (1984). Conferencing: The psychodynamics of teaching contraries. *The Writing Center Journal, 4*(2), 22–30.

LeBlanc, P., Hawisher, G., Selfe, C., & Moran, C. (1996). *Computers and the teaching of writing in American higher education, 1979-1994: A history.* Norwood, NJ: Ablex.

Levin, R. (1984). Computer-assisted writing. In D. Dellow & L. Poole (Eds.), *New directions in community colleges* . San Francisco: Jossey-Bass.

Little, S. (1987). The computer as audience: Using HOMER, a text analysis program. *Computers and Composition, 4*(2), 106–120.

Lochman, D. (1986). Play and games: Implications for the writing center. *The Writing Center Journal, 7*(1), 11–18.

Lundsford, A. (1991). Collaboration, control, and the idea of the writing center. *The Writing Center Journal, 12*(1), 3–10.

Lynch, R. (1988). Two useful programs for english as a second language and english students. *Collegiate Microcomputer, 5*(1), 70–71.

Marcus, S. (1984). Real-time gadgets with feedback: Special effects iin computer-assisted writing. In W. Wresch (Ed.), *The computer in composition instruction: A writer's tool* (pp. 120–130). Urbana, IL: NCTE.

McCann, T. (1984). Sentence combining for the microcomputer. *Computers and Composition, 1*(3), 1–2.

Melnick, J. (1984). The politics of writing conferences: Describing authority through speech act theory. *The Writing Center Journal, 4*(2), 9–21.

Miller, S. (1989). *Rescuing the subject: A critical introduction to rhetoric and the writer.* Carbondale: Southern Illinois University Press.

Miller, S. (1991). *Textual carnivals: The politics of composition.* Carbondale, IL: Southern Illinois University Press.

Moran, C. (1992). Computers and the writing classroom: A look to the future. In G. Hawisher and P. LeBlanc (Eds.) *Re-imagining computers and composition: Teaching and research in the virtual age* (pp. 7–23). Portsmouth, NH: Boynton/Cook Publishers.

Moseley, A. (1984). From factory to workshop: Revising the writing center. *The Writing Center Journal, 4*(2), 31–38.

Murray, D. (1976). Teach writing as a process not product. In R. Graves (Ed.), *Rhetoric and composition: A sourcebook for teachers* (pp. 79–82). Rochelle Park: Hayden Book Company, Inc.

Neuwirth, C., Kaufer, D., & Geisler, C. (1984). What is EPISTLE? *Computers and Composition, 1*(4), 1–2.

Nigliazzo, M. (1982). Audiovisual instruction in a writing laboratory. In Muriel Harris (Ed.), *Tutoring writing: A sourcebook for writing labs* (pp. 147–152). Glenview, IL: Scott, Foresman and Company.

Nold, E. (1975). Fear and trembling: The humanist approaches the computer. *College Composition and Communication, 26*, 269–273.

North, S. (1979). *Writing centers: A sourcebook.* Unpublished doctoral dissertation, University at Albany, State University of New York.

North, S. (1982). Writing center diagnosis: The composing profile. In M. Harris (Ed.), *Tutoring writing: A sourcebook for writing labs* (pp. 42–52). Glenview, IL: Scott, Foresman and Co.

North, S. (1984). The idea of a writing center. *College English, 46*(5), 433–446.

North, S. (1987). *The making of knowledge in composition: Portrait of an emerging field.* Upper Montclair, NJ: Boynton/Cook.

North, S. (1994). Revisiting "the idea of the writing center." *The Writing Center Journal, 15*(1), 7–19.

Norton, D., & Hansen, K. (1982). The potential of computer-assisted instruction in writing labs. In M. Harris (Ed.), *Tutoring writing: A sourcebook for writing labs* (pp. 153–163). Glenview, IL: Scott, Foresman and Co.

Nuguyen, K. (1995). Gilman: A new perspective on Emersonian ideas. *American Literature Survey Site* [online]. Path: http://www.cwrl.utexas.edu/~nick/evans/firstpapers/knguyenpaper. html

Ohmann, R. (1976). Literacy, technology, and monopoly capital. *College English, 47*(7), 675–689.

Ohman, R. (1985). *English in America: A radical view of the profession.* Hanover: Wesleyan University Press.

Ong, W. (1982). *Orality and literacy: The technologizing of the word.* New York: Routledge.

Pagliaro, L. (1983). The history and development of CAI: 1926–1981, An overview. *The Alberta Journal of Educational Research, 29*(1), 75–84.

Pappert, S. (1987). Computer criticism vs. technocentric thinking. *Educational Researcher, 16,* 22–30.

Pratt, M. L. (1991). Arts of the Contact Zone. *Profession, 91,* 33–40. New York: Modern Language Association.

Readings, B. (1996). *The university in ruins.* Cambridge, MA: Harvard University Press.

Rodrigues, D., & Rodrigues, R. (1984). Computer-based invention: It's place and potentional. *College Composition and Communication, 35,* 78–87.

Romano, S. (1993). The egalistarianism narrative: Whose story? Which yardstick? *Computers and Composition, 10*(3), 5–28.

Roy, E. (1993). Computerized scoring of placement exams: A validation. *Journal of Basic Writing, 12*(2), 41–54.

Russell, D. (1991). *Writing in the academic disciplines, 1870–1990: A curricular history.* Carbondale: Southern Illinois University Press.

Scharton, M., & Neuleib, J. (1990). Tutors and computers, an easy alliance. *Writing Center Journal, 11*(1), 49–58.

Schwartz, H. (1984). SEEN: A tutorial and user network for hypothesis testing. In William Wresch (Ed.),*The computer in composition instruction: A writer's tool* (pp. 47–62). Urbana, IL: National Council of Teachers of English.

Schwartz, H. (1990). Ethical considerations of educational computer use. In D. Holdstein and C. Selfe (Eds.), *Computers and writing: Theory, research, practice* (pp. 18–30). New York: Modern Language Association.

Sirc, G., & Reynolds, T. (1993). Seeing students as writers. In Bertram Bruce, J. Peyton, & T. Batson (Eds.) *Network-based writing classrooms: Promises and realities*, (pp. 138–160). New York: Cambridge University Press.

Skinner, B.F. (1964). Why we need teaching machines. In J. DeCecco (Ed.), *Educational technology: Readings in programmed instruction* (pp. 92–112). New York: Holt, Rinehart and Winston.

Southwell, M. (1984). The COMP-LAB writing modules: Computer-assisted grammar instruction. In W. Wresch (Ed.), *The computer in composition instruction: A writer's tool* (pp. 91–104). Urbana, IL: National Council of Teachers English.

Sternglass, M. (1997). *Time to know them: A longitudinal study of writing and learning at the college level.* Mahwah, NJ: Erlbaum.

Stillman, P. (1985). A writer (and teacher of writing) confronts word processing. In J. Collins & E. Sommers (Eds.),*Writing on-line: Using computers in the teaching of writing* (pp. 19–28). Upper Montclair, NJ: Boynton/Cook.

Strickland, J. (1985). Prewriting and computing. In J. Collins & E. Sommers (Eds.), *Writing on-line: Using computers in the teaching of writing* (pp. 67–74). Upper Montclair, NJ: Boynton/Cook.

Strickland, J. (1986). Computers, invention, and the power to change student writing (CS 209 643). *U.S. Department of Education*. (ERIC Document Reproduction Service No. ED 267 449.

Stuckey, J. E. (1991). *The violence of literacy*. Portsmouth, NH: Boynton/Cook.

Summerfield, J. (1988).Writing centers: A long view. *The Writing Center Journal, 8*(2), 3–10.

Thomas, J., & Wimett, E. (1984). Logicomp project description. *Computers and Composition, 1*(3), 13.

Trimbur, J. (1987). Peer tutoring: A contradiction in terms. *Writing Center Journal , 7*(2), 21–28.

Trimbur, J. (1991). Literacy and the discourse of crisis. In R. Bullock, C. Schuster, & J. Trimbur (Eds.) *The politics of writing instruction: Postsecondary* (pp. 277–296). Portsmouth, NH: Boynton/Cook.

Vasile, K., & Ghizzone, N. (1992). Computer integrated tutoring. *The Writing Lab Newsletter , 16*(9–10), 17–19.

Veit, R. (1979). Are machines the answer? *The Writing Lab Newsletter, 4*(4), 1–2.

Warnock, J., & Warnock, T. (1984). Liberatory writing centers: Restoring authority to writers. In Gary Olson (Ed.), *Writing Centers: Theory and Administration* (pp. 3–15). Urbana, IL: National Council of Teachers of English.

Welch, N. (1993). On student's many voices: Reading, writing, and responding with Bakhtin. *Journal of Advanced Composition, 13*(2), 493–502.

Welch, N. (1993). From silence to noise: The writing center as critical exile. *The Writing Center Journal, 14*(1), 3–15.

Welch, N. (1997). *Getting restless: Rethinking revision in writing instruction*. Portsmouth: Boynton/Cook.

Williams, R. (1998). No march on Washington. *Intertext*, 6 [online]. Path: http://wrt.syr.edu/wrt/pub/intertext/VI/williams.html

Wittig, S., & Bracewell, M. (1975). Evaluating CAI in English. *Proceedings of Conference on Computers in the Undergraduate Curricula*. Fort Worth, TX: Texas Christian University.

Wresch, W. (1984). Introduction. In W. Wresch (Ed.), *The computer in composition instruction: A writer's tool* (pp. 1–12). Urbana, IL: National Council of Teachers of English.

Yahner, W., & Murdick, W. (1991). The evolution of a writing center: 1972–1990. *The Writing Center Journal, 11*(2), 13–28.

Zoellner, R. (1969). Talk-write: A behavioral pedagogy for composition. *College English, 30*(4), 267–320.

Author Index

Subject Index